Si King & Dave Myers

THE HAIRY
DIETERS

MAKE IT EASY

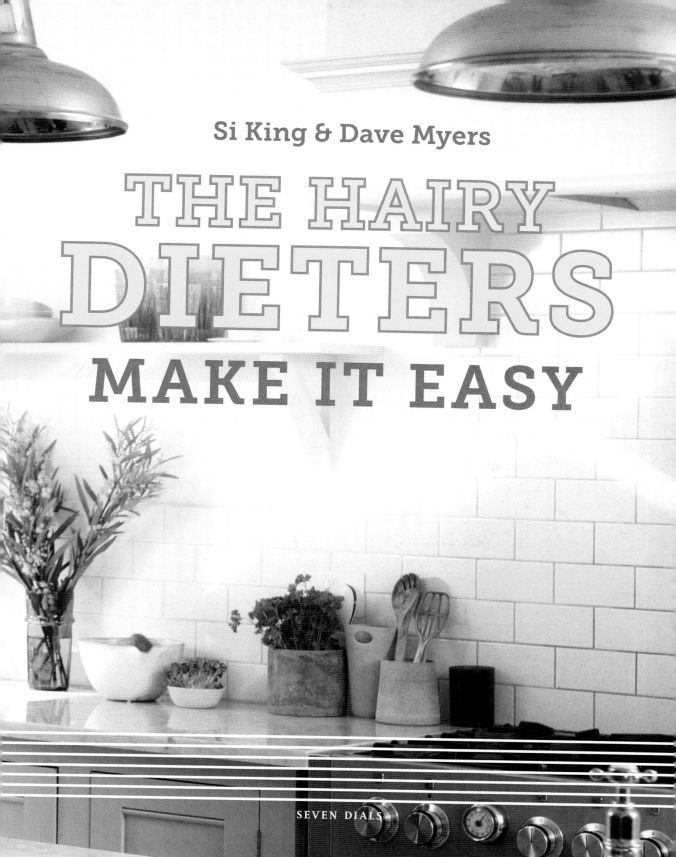

Si King & Dave Myers

THE HAIRY DIETERS
MAKE IT EASY

SEVEN DIALS

CONTENTS

WELCOME TO MAKE IT EASY

Believe us, we know as well as anybody that dieting is hard. This book is filled with our winning tips on how to make losing weight as easy, delicious and filling as possible!

The aim of this book is to make life and weight loss just that bit easier. These recipes will help you shed the pounds and you'll eat well in the process. Remember – low-cal doesn't have to mean low-taste. This food is fantastic.

We love food and cooking and, in the bad old days, we thought that meant dieting would mean misery. Now, thanks to working on our Hairy Dieters books, we know better – you can cook great food, enjoy eating, feel full and still lose weight.

We've both struggled with busy schedules and weight loss goals. We understand the pressures of modern life and we know that lots of us find it hard to make time for cooking. Our hope is that you will use this book on a daily basis and so we've taken care to make the recipes as simple and no-fuss as possible. As always, though, they deliver on taste – and they will help you keep your weight on track.

THE COLD HARD FACTS

We've learned the hard way that the sooner you face up to weight problems the better. They're not going to go away by themselves. You have to change your lifestyle. And the real challenge is keeping the weight off once you've lost it. Maintaining a healthy weight really is vital. It's not just about being 'beach body ready'! Every day we hear more and more about the effect that being overweight has on your health. We have to shed the fat and ditch it for good.

Now for once we're going to get serious. It's scary facing up to the truth and we all want to bury our heads in the sand, but these are the cold hard facts from the NHS.

Being overweight or obese increases the risk of many serious illnesses, such as type 2 diabetes, high blood pressure, heart disease and strokes, as well as cancer. Obesity has been blamed for about 30,000 deaths a year in the UK – 9,000 of those taking place before retirement age.

The latest research from the World Health Organisation warns that being overweight or obese is the most important avoidable cause of cancer after tobacco. A study has shown links between excess weight and ten types of cancer, including bowel, kidney and cervical, and estimates that weight problems are behind about 18,000 cases of cancer a year in the UK.

KEEPING THE WEIGHT OFF

Fad diets that whack the weight off quickly are all very well, but if you then go back to your old ways you will just put it all on again – and more. Yo-yo diets are a risk to health and self esteem. It's much better to lose weight by slow, steady changes rather than by cutting out whole food groups or adopting weird ways of eating, neither of which are sustainable in the long run.

Weight loss is all about calories in and calories out .You can lose weight by restricting your calorie intake or by burning more calories, but the best way is to do a bit of both – small changes to diet combined with some exercise. This doesn't have to mean going to the gym. Just get off the sofa and move – and that can be walking, cycling, dancing, playing a sport you love, whatever takes your fancy. The main thing is to find some exercise you enjoy. If you do, you are more likely to do it and keep doing it. Simple innit!

And once you've lost the weight, keep a check on the scales. It's much better to address any issues when you're a kilo or so over than to let it creep up to five or ten or more. If, when you go to buy new clothes or look out your summer gear, you find stuff mysteriously doesn't fit any more, don't automatically settle for a bigger size. Face facts, be honest with yourself and do something about it. We know it's easier said than done but this book is here to help.

QUICK AND EASY COOKING

We've taken the faff out of food in these recipes so you can cook great meals that will help you lose weight. Each recipe is calorie counted so you can control your portions. It is very hard to estimate the number of calories in a dish just by looking at it – even nutritionists get it wrong.

If you cook your own meals you know exactly what's in them. We're learning more and more about the possible dangers to our health of eating too much heavily processed food. Cooking your own has to be the way to go. Recent research has shown that we buy a huge amount of ultra-processed food in this country – food that is barely recognisable as food. The best way to avoid this is to cook your own, using ingredients that have had as little done to them as possible. These recipes show that it can be done and we've made them as easy as we can so you can achieve your goals and stay healthy

Having a well-stocked fridge, freezer and store cupboard is a great help. If you have good stuff available to make healthy food you're less likely to be tempted to eat a ready meal or a takeaway. Make sure you eat plenty of fresh veg and don't assume that anything in a can or packet is bad for you. Frozen veg are fine, as are canned tomatoes and beans, cooked lentils and so on. Some little cheats work brilliantly; just don't buy them from the chippy.

THOSE LOVELY VEG

We learned so much about cooking veg when we wrote our *Go Veggie* book and, although we're not vegetarians, veg play a big part in our diet. Vegetables are your best friends when you're trying to eat healthily. Most are fat-free and low in calories, and they add fibre (a nutrient most of us don't eat enough of), vitamins, minerals and phytochemicals to our diet. And for anyone trying to lose weight, there's another big advantage: veg bulk out a meal and make it more satisfying and filling. Think of it this way, the longer food takes to digest, the longer it keeps you full!

We all should be eating at least five portions of veg and fruit a day – preferably more. As always, we've included plenty of veg in the recipes in this book, but an extra helping of most types of vegetable makes very little difference to the calorie counts. Don't be shy about eating vegetables and get in the habit of throwing a handful of extra veg – such as peas, sweetcorn or beans – into your meal and serve extra greens on the side. It's easy peasy.

Just look at these – all the calorie counts below are for one 80 gram serving:

BROCCOLI: 27 CALORIES • **PEAS:** 76 CALORIES • **GREEN BEANS:** 28 CALORIES
CARROTS: 34 CALORIES • **CAULIFLOWER:** 26 CALORIES • **COURGETTE:** 18 CALORIES
SWEETCORN: 68 CALORIES • **½ RED PEPPER:** 21 CALORIES

DRINKS – HMMM!

Now, this is a tough one for us, but we do know willpower dissolves in alcohol. After a drink or two everyone is more prone to overeating so you do need to make an effort not to drink too much when you're dieting. In one experiment in the States, some students were invited to eat what they wanted from a buffet on two separate occasions – the first time after drinking non-alcoholic beers and the second after drinking alcoholic beers. They took more food, with poorer food choices, after drinking alcohol.

Diet drinks are calorie-free but they are still very sweet so they don't help you re-educate your taste buds or change your body's craving for sweet stuff. They rot your teeth too. If you really want something other than water, a little squash with fizzy water is better than a diet drink.

COOKING FOR REAL LIFE

We've learned so much over the years and we want to pass this on to you. This is more than a cookbook – it's a manual for real life cooking and eating. You don't have to give up potatoes, pasta, even pudding. Just eat wisely, having more of the good stuff and less of the bad. Even non-dieters will be happy with these recipes and they can have extra carbs or bigger portions if they need them.

We've thought about the way we live and the way we eat. Each chapter in the book is designed to make life and weight loss easier. The first chapter is filled with recipes that you can make in 15 minutes flat – ideal for times when you're hungry and need to get good healthy food on the table fast. Another chapter contains recipes with only six ingredients or fewer – easy to shop, easy to cook. There are chapters on one-pot wonders – everyone's favourites – and on assembly job meals that are more about simply putting ingredients together rather than cooking. A chapter on batch cooking shows you how to make the most of ingredients, such as a Sunday roast, and includes recipes that you can make in quantity and freeze to save both time and money. And because we all need a treat sometimes, there are some easy peasy puds.

You dont have to give up potatoes, pasta, or even pudding. You eat wisely and give these easy recipes a whirl.

DAVE: I love food and cooking – I wake up thinking about what to make for supper – and that's both a blessing and a curse. My problem is that when I'm away from home I find it hard to stick to my regime and it's all too easy to binge on high-cal food. At home, I take control, and I find that by using our Hairy Dieter recipes I can maintain a healthy weight and still enjoy my meals. Even then, I get tempted to eat what I shouldn't – and that's where the recipes in this book come in. I want things I can make quickly and easily.

With a bit of planning you can always have something tasty and satisfying on the table. Use your freezer and look at the batch-cooking chapter in this book for ideas. Curries, soups and stews all freeze well so make a big batch when you have time.

SI: My boys have fled the nest, so I often find myself cooking just for one, which makes it easier to resist temptation. My answer is simply not to buy the stuff I know I shouldn't be eating and that's easier now I'm on my own. The question I ask myself when I finish my meal is 'Am I satisfied?' and usually the answer is 'Yes'. If I don't do this, I'm tempted to go on eating.

The hard part is alcohol. I like to have a glass of wine with my evening meal and I find it difficult to break that habit when I'm dieting. It's an effort and my body has learned to expect that drink. But it's not impossible and it doesn't last forever. I make it easier on myself by crying quietly into a handkerchief. No, only joking! I move all the booze into the shed. If I want a drink I've gotta go out to get it and I never do!

Sometimes what you most need to keep your weight down is to get the right food on the table – fast and with no fuss – before you start snacking.
The recipes in this chapter are lifesavers, as they can be made in 15 minutes or less. Make sure you have all the ingredients to hand though. The 15 minutes doesn't include you popping to the shops to buy an onion!

15-MINUTE FILLERS

CHICKPEA AND PANEER FRITTATA

Paneer is a fresh white cheese that's very popular in India and readily available in the UK. It's made without rennet so is perfect if you're vegetarian, and it works well in this Italian-style omelette or frittata. This is great as a starter with a dollop of mango chutney on the side or you can serve it with salad as a light main course or a brunch dish. Good cold in a lunchbox too.

1 tsp olive oil
1 onion, sliced
20g fresh root ginger, finely chopped
400g can of chickpeas, drained and rinsed
2 tsp curry powder
small bunch of coriander, chopped, plus extra to garnish
6 eggs, beaten
100g paneer, diced

Heat the olive oil in a large, non-stick frying pan or an omelette pan. Add the onion slices and cook them over a medium to high heat, turning them regularly, until they're just starting to brown. They don't need to soften much and should still have some texture.

Add the ginger to the pan and cook for another minute, then add the chickpeas. Add the curry powder and stir to combine, then sprinkle over the chopped coriander.

Pour in the eggs, swirling them round so they are distributed evenly in the pan, then dot the paneer over the top. Cook for 3–4 minutes until the underside of the frittata has set and browned lightly – you will see the colour change around the edges. Meanwhile, heat your grill to a medium setting.

Put the pan under the grill and finish off the cooking. The eggs and paneer will brown lightly and the frittata will puff up a little.

Remove the pan from the grill and leave the frittata to drop down again, then cut it into wedges. Serve hot or cold, garnished with a few extra coriander leaves.

QUICK MEXICAN EGGS

This Mexican feast – known as huevos rancheros or ranchers' eggs – is one of our very favourites for breakfast, brunch or any time of day really! Proper refried beans take a while but our super-quick version is ready in minutes and we think beans are the dieters' best friend.

Beans
1 tsp olive oil
1 garlic clove, crushed
1 tsp oregano
1 tsp ground cumin
1 tbsp tomato purée
400g can of black beans, drained but not rinsed
sea salt and black pepper

Salsa
juice of 1 lime
1 avocado, flesh diced

To serve
4 corn tortillas
low-cal oil spray
4 eggs
½ tsp smoked chilli powder
small bunch of coriander, chopped

First prepare the beans. Heat the olive oil in a small saucepan and add the garlic. Cook for 30 seconds, then add the oregano, cumin and tomato purée. Continue to cook until the purée starts to separate, then add the beans along with 100ml of water. Season the beans with salt and pepper and leave them to simmer gently while you get everything else ready.

For the salsa, put the lime juice in a bowl with half a teaspoon of salt, then add the avocado and stir to combine.

Now warm the tortillas. Sprinkle each tortilla with water and place it in a dry frying pan for 10–15 seconds, then flip and repeat. Wrap the tortillas in a tea towel to keep them warm.

Spritz a frying pan with oil. Add the eggs and fry them gently until they are cooked as you like them. Sprinkle each one with a little chilli powder.

Divide the beans between 4 plates and top with the eggs. Serve with the tortillas and salsa and garnish with plenty of chopped coriander. That's it!

HAIRY BIKER TIP: If you like, add a bag of baby spinach leaves to the beans, stirring them through until the leaves wilt – really good.

PRAWN FOO YUNG

This is just the job when you're hungry and want to eat something fast to stop yourself snacking! No need to go to the takeaway for a quick fix when you can knock up this healthy version in less time than it takes to queue. Get your ingredients prepped first, you can use a food processor if you're not a great chopper, and the rest is a doddle.

4 eggs

1 tsp soy sauce

a few drops of sesame oil

½ tsp Chinese five-spice powder

100g raw peeled prawns, roughly chopped

1 medium carrot (about 75g), cut into matchsticks

¼ small white cabbage (about 100g), shredded

2 spring onions, finely sliced into rounds

5g fresh root ginger, finely chopped or grated

small bunch of coriander, roughly chopped

1 tsp vegetable oil

sea salt and black pepper

Beat the eggs in a bowl with the soy sauce, sesame oil and five-spice. Season well with salt and pepper. Stir in the prawns, vegetables, fresh ginger and coriander and mix thoroughly.

Preheat your grill to its highest setting. Add the vegetable oil to a non-stick pan and place it on the hob. When the pan is very hot, add the egg mixture, making sure it is evenly spread out over the base of the pan. Press it down lightly, then cook until the underside is a rich golden brown.

To finish, place the pan under the grill for 3–4 minutes until the prawns are completely cooked through. Serve immediately.

HAIRY BIKER TIP: We sometimes add bean sprouts to the mixture for a bit of extra low-cal bulk.

SALMON AND SWEETCORN FRITTERS

Fresh salmon is packed with protein and healthy oils and makes a mega-tasty fritter.
These are a great snack or starter or you can serve them with a salad for a light meal.
They're just right for packing into a lunchbox too.

3 eggs
1 tbsp soy sauce
150g sweetcorn (defrosted
if frozen)
150g fresh salmon
fillet, skinned and diced
small bunch of coriander,
finely chopped
60g plain flour
low-cal oil spray
(preferably sunflower)
sea salt and black pepper

Dipping sauce
2 tbsp soy sauce
juice of 1 lime
1 tsp hot chilli sauce

Put a large frying pan on the hob to heat up while you make the fritter batter.

Crack the eggs into a large bowl, add the soy sauce and season with salt and pepper. Beat the eggs well, then add the sweetcorn, salmon and coriander. Sprinkle over the flour and stir well to combine.

Spray the frying pan with oil and add 4 ladlefuls of batter, well spread out. Cook the fritters for up to 2 minutes until the undersides are nicely browned, then flip them over and continue to fry for another minute until just cooked. Remove the fritters from the pan and keep them warm. Spray the pan with more oil and make the second batch in the same way.

Mix the soy sauce and lime juice with the chilli sauce and serve it with the fritters as a dipping sauce.

Serves 4 | 233 calories per serving | **Prep and cooking time:** 15 minutes

CORONATION CHICKEN SALAD

This makes a fab lunchbox dish as well as an easy meal and it's a very adaptable recipe. For example, you can add some new potatoes if you fancy a bit more bulk. We love the peppery flavour of good old-fashioned mustard cress but you can use coriander instead – or as well – if you like.

200g fine beans,
tops trimmed
150g low-fat
Greek-style yoghurt
1 tbsp curry powder
1 tbsp mango chutney
small bunch of coriander
300g cooked
chicken, diced
4 little gem lettuces,
roughly torn
½ cucumber, diced
4 spring onions, sliced
into rounds
2 tbsp flaked almonds
mustard cress
pinch of cayenne
(optional)
sea salt and black pepper

Bring a saucepan of water to the boil and season with salt. Add the beans and cook them for 3–4 minutes until just done but still a nice deep green colour. Drain the beans and plunge them into cold water to cool. Set them aside.

For the coronation chicken, put the yoghurt in a bowl with the curry powder and mango chutney. Season with salt and pepper, then stir to combine. Add the coriander and the chicken and fold through.

Tip the chicken into a salad bowl and thin it slightly with 2 or 3 tablespoons of water. Add the green beans, little gems, cucumber and spring onions and toss everything lightly, so the salad leaves are nicely coated in the dressing.

Put the flaked almonds in a dry frying pan and toast them until they are light golden brown and aromatic. Tip them on to a plate and leave to cool slightly, then sprinkle them over the salad. Top the salad with a few cress leaves and sprinkle with cayenne if you fancy a little more heat. Serve immediately.

HAIRY BIKER TIP: This is a great thing to do with leftover roast chicken. Her Majesty would approve! Good in a wrap too.

TURKISH TURKEY FLATBREADS

A flavour sensation, this is our version of a popular Turkish flatbread dish called lahmacun, made super-quick by using pitta breads. We also like to use turkey mince instead of the traditional lamb, as it is lower in fat but still tastes great.

2 pitta breads
200g turkey mince
1 tsp ground cumin
½ tsp paprika or Turkish pepper flakes
¼ tsp ground cinnamon
½ small onion, finely chopped or grated
1 garlic clove, crushed
2 tbsp tomato purée
2 tbsp finely chopped parsley
10g pine nuts
sea salt and black pepper

To serve
handful of rocket leaves
lemon wedges

Preheat the oven to its highest setting. Cut the pittas in half to make 4 flat pieces of bread.

Put the turkey mince in a bowl and add the cumin, paprika or pepper flakes, the cinnamon, onion, garlic, tomato purée and parsley. Season well with salt and pepper, then mix thoroughly to make a thick red paste.

Spread the mixture over the pittas, making sure you push it right to the edges, then top with some pine nuts. Place the pittas on a baking tray and bake them in the preheated oven for 7–8 minutes until the meat is very lightly charred and cooked through.

Sprinkle a few rocket leaves over each flatbread and serve them immediately with lemon wedges.

PEA, MINT AND HAM SOUP

Frozen peas are such a great product and perfect for making a quick and satisfying soup. Pea and mint is a top soup anyway in our opinion, but this crispy ham garnish turns it into something really special. And it's so quick to make!

10g butter

bunch of spring onions, finely shredded

2 garlic cloves, crushed

500g frozen peas

2 tsp dried mint or a small bunch of fresh, shredded

1 litre vegetable or chicken stock

sea salt and black pepper

Ham garnish

1 tsp olive oil

1 tsp wholegrain mustard

½ tsp honey

100g cooked ham, shredded

Heat the butter in a saucepan. Add the spring onions and cook them for a couple of minutes until they're starting to soften, then add the garlic. Cook for a further 2 minutes, then stir in the peas and mint. Season with salt and pepper, then pour in the stock. Bring to the boil, then turn down the heat and leave the soup to simmer for 5 minutes.

Meanwhile, make the ham garnish. Heat the olive oil in a small frying pan. Add the mustard and honey and stir until the honey has melted. Add the ham and stir to coat it with the contents of the pan. Fry the ham over a medium high heat until it's all crisp and browned.

Blitz the pea soup until smooth with stick blender or in a jug blender. Serve garnished with the crispy ham.

SPEEDY TURKEY CHILLI

We love this low-cal chilli made with turkey mince – great with tortillas, rice or cauliflower rice (see page 180). And if you want a veggie version, leave out the turkey and add 300g of cooked lentils instead. This is better than adding more beans, as it gives the chilli more texture. You could also make the chilli with quorn if you're a fan.

1 tsp olive oil
bunch of spring onions, sliced into rounds
1 red pepper, diced
small bunch of coriander
300g turkey mince
1 tsp ground cumin
1 tsp garlic powder or granules
½ tsp ground cinnamon
1 tbsp tomato purée
1–2 tsp chipotle paste
400g can of black beans, drained but not rinsed
150g sweetcorn
lime wedges
sea salt and black pepper

(Best to freeze without the coriander leaves.)

Heat the olive oil in a large saucepan. Add the spring onions and red pepper and fry them over a high heat for 2 minutes. Finely chop the coriander stems, reserving the leaves for later, and add the stems to the saucepan together with the turkey mince. Continue to cook over a high heat, stirring constantly, for another 2 minutes.

Add the spices, tomato purée and chipotle paste and stir to combine. Then add the beans and sweetcorn along with 150ml of water and season with salt and pepper. Simmer for 5 minutes until the sauce has thickened without being dry.

Serve sprinkled with plenty of chopped coriander leaves and a squeeze of lime. A salad on the side is nice too.

HAIRY BIKER TIP: For speedy chopping of the spring onions, bunch them all together, then trim and then slice them all at the same time.

PORK STROGANOFF

Creamy and delicious, this seems quite a fancy dish — not like diet food at all — but it's one of the quickest suppers we know. Pork medallions are neat little slices of pork fillet and you'll find them in supermarkets. They're low in fat but high in protein so a good healthy meat.

2 tsp olive oil

1 onion, thinly sliced

200g mushrooms, thinly sliced

500g pork medallions or steaks, trimmed of all fat and thinly sliced into strips

1 heaped tsp sweet smoked paprika

200ml pork, beef or chicken stock or water

75ml half-fat crème fraiche

2 tbsp chopped parsley leaves

sea salt and black pepper

Heat a teaspoon of the oil in a large frying pan. Add the onion and mushrooms and fry them over a high heat for 5 minutes until they are well browned and starting to soften. Transfer them to a plate.

Add the remaining oil to the pan. Season the pork with salt and pepper, then add it to the pan. Fry quickly, stirring until the meat has browned on all sides.

Put the onion and mushrooms back in the pan. Sprinkle over the paprika and stir, then pour over the stock or water. Bring to the boil and then simmer until the pork is cooked through and the liquid has reduced by about half.

Stir in the crème fraiche and heat until the stroganoff is piping hot without letting it come to the boil.

Sprinkle with parsley and serve with a big pile of greens.

THAI TURKEY MINCE SALAD

Inspired by the Thai dish known as laab, this is a salad that packs a punch. It makes a great lunch and it's ideal for piling into a box and taking to work with you. You could also spoon the salad on to lettuce leaves and serve it as a starter if you like.

Salad

1 large carrot, grated

150g Chinese or white cabbage, shredded

bunch of spring onions, sliced into rounds

8 radishes, sliced

Turkey

2 tsp vegetable oil

15g fresh root ginger, grated

2 garlic cloves, crushed

2 red chillies, finely chopped

400g turkey mince

zest of 1 lime and juice of 1–2 limes

1–2 tbsp fish sauce

sea salt and black pepper

To serve

small bunch of coriander

handful of mint leaves

Put the carrot, cabbage, spring onions and radishes in a salad bowl and toss them all together.

Heat the vegetable oil in a frying pan and add the ginger, garlic and chillies. Fry them all for a minute or so until you can smell their wonderful aroma, then add the turkey mince. Season with salt and pepper, then continue to cook until the turkey has browned.

Add the lime zest and the juice of one lime along with a tablespoon of fish sauce and stir them into the mince. Cook for another couple of minutes until the turkey is completely cooked through. Taste and add more lime juice and fish sauce if you need to.

Pour the mince mixture over the salad and stir it in. Garnish with the coriander and mint leaves. Serve the salad warm, or prepare it ahead and serve it at room temperature.

BIKER BURGERS

In the end we think that the best burgers are made with just meat and seasoning. We all love a juicy burger with a bun, but when you're counting the calories why not wrap everything up in crunchy lettuce leaves instead? You get all the great taste without the stodge. Genius!

400g lean beef mince
low-cal oil spray
4 large lettuce leaves
2 medium tomatoes, sliced
8 thin slices of cucumber, cut on the diagonal
8 thin rounds of red onion
sea salt and black pepper

To serve
mustard or low-cal mayonnaise

Season the meat with plenty of salt and pepper and mix thoroughly. Divide the meat into 4 equal portions, then shape these into patties about 2cm thick.

Spray a non-stick frying pan or griddle with oil and place it over the heat. When the pan is too hot to hold your hand over, add the burgers. Leave them for 4 minutes – by this point the undersides should have developed a crust and be well seared. Flip them over and cook on the other side for 3 minutes for a rare burger, 4 minutes for a medium-rare burger, 5 minutes for a medium burger and 6 for well done.

Leave the burgers to rest for a couple of minutes. To assemble, take a lettuce leaf and place a slice of tomato, cucumber and red onion on one half of it. Top with a burger, then add another slice each of tomato, cucumber and red onion. Add any mayonnaise or mustard, then fold the other half of the lettuce leaf over the burger and vegetables. Repeat to make the rest of the burgers.

Eat immediately.

These recipes are really about
putting good, tasty ingredients
together, with very little effort,
to make something truly delicious.
Great at the end of a long day.
Some involve cooking just one item
while others need no cooking at all,
just chopping, slicing and serving.

ASSEMBLY JOBS

HALLOUMI AND VEGETABLE SKEWERS

Halloumi is a Cypriot cheese that's in every supermarket now and you can even get a light, reduced-calorie version. It's great cooked and these colourful skewers make a tasty starter or you can serve them with a salad for a more substantial meal.

225g light halloumi cheese, cut into 16 cubes

8 button mushrooms

½ red pepper, cut into 8 pieces

½ green pepper, cut into 8 pieces

1 courgette, cut into 8 rounds

1 red onion, cut into 8 wedges

low-cal oil spray

1 tsp dried oregano

sea salt and black pepper

To serve

cayenne or chilli powder (optional)

lemon wedges

Preheat the oven to 200°C/Fan 180°C/Gas 6. Thread the pieces of halloumi and vegetables on to 8 skewers, making sure you get a nice mix on each one. Place them on a baking tray, then spray them with oil. Season with salt and pepper and sprinkle over the oregano.

Bake the skewers in the oven for 15 minutes, turning them over once halfway through the cooking time so they cook evenly. The vegetables should be very succulent and slightly charred, but still with some bite to them, and the halloumi should be well browned.

Serve sprinkled with a little cayenne or chilli powder if you like and some lemon wedges to squeeze over.

HAIRY BIKER TIP: You could also cook these on a barbecue or a griddle pan. They will take 3–4 minutes on each side. They'd be great packed into pitta bread too, but watch the calories.

CAULIFLOWER TANDOORI

Cauliflower goes beautifully with tandoori flavours and makes a great low-cal alternative to meat. Partner this with some pitta, hummus and yoghurt dip and you have a feast.

2 tbsp tandoori paste (shop-bought or see p.181)
100ml low-fat yoghurt
juice of 1 lemon
1 medium cauliflower, cut into small florets
low-cal oil spray, preferably olive
sea salt and black pepper

Yoghurt dip
200ml low-fat yoghurt
1 tsp dried mint

To serve
4 pitta breads (shop-bought or see p.178)
4 tbsp reduced-fat hummus
small bunch of coriander or parsley
lemon wedges

Preheat the oven to 200°C/Fan 180°C/Gas 6. Put the tandoori paste, yoghurt and lemon juice in a large bowl and season with salt and pepper. Mix thoroughly, then add the cauliflower. Stir to make sure the cauliflower is completely coated in the sauce, then transfer it to a roasting tin.

Add 100ml of water to the tin and spritz the cauliflower with oil. Roast the cauli in the oven for 30–40 minutes until cooked through and lightly charred in places.

For the dip, mix the yoghurt and mint in a bowl and season with salt and pepper.

Warm the pittas in a toaster or on a griddle. Slit each one down the side to make a pocket and carefully spread one half with hummus. Fill each pocket with some cauliflower, then top with a drizzle of minted yoghurt and some coriander or parsley. Serve with a squeeze of lemon.

HAIRY BIKER TIP: You could also make the tandoori mixture with tandoori powder, which is a great thing to have in your store cupboard. Just mix the powder with the yoghurt and lemon juice and use as above.

ROASTED VEGETABLE GREEK SALAD

Everyone loves a traditional Greek salad, piled high with delicious tomatoes, olives and feta cheese. We've boosted the usual recipe by roasting the pepper and onions and adding some chickpeas to make a hearty meal, packed with veg and goodness.

1 green pepper, cut into strips

1 red onion, cut into fine wedges

1 tsp olive oil

2 tsp dried oregano

1 cos lettuce, shredded

½ cucumber, halved lengthways and sliced into crescents

4 tomatoes, cut into fine wedges

400g can of chickpeas, drained and rinsed

150g feta cheese, crumbled

50g black olives, sliced

sea salt and black pepper

Dressing
1 tbsp olive oil
1 tsp red wine vinegar

Preheat the oven to 200°C/Fan 180°C/Gas 6. Put the pepper and onion on a roasting tray and drizzle them with the olive oil. Season generously and sprinkle over half the oregano. Roast the veg in the oven for 20 minutes, until they are browned slightly but still have some bite to them. Remove and leave them to cool to room temperature.

Arrange the cos lettuce in a salad bowl or on a platter and top with the cucumber, followed by the tomatoes. Sprinkle over the chickpeas, then top with the roasted green pepper and red onion, the feta and the olives.

Whisk the oil and vinegar to make the dressing and pour it over the salad, then finish with the remaining oregano. Serve at room temperature.

CHOPPED SALAD
WITH BLUE CHEESE DRESSING

The ingredients in this American-style salad are chopped small, to a more or less uniform size, which makes it pleasing to the eye and easy to eat. The blue cheese dressing continues the US vibe and makes this a super-tasty salad to serve with something like the halloumi skewers on page 38. Check that your blue cheese is suitable for vegetarians.

2 little gems, or 1 cos lettuce, shredded

½ cucumber, diced

3 celery sticks, diced

1 carrot, cut into short matchsticks

6 radishes, diced

100g cherry tomatoes, cut into quarters

bunch of spring onions, sliced into rounds

leaves from 2 sprigs of tarragon, finely chopped

½ punnet of mustard cress

sea salt and black pepper

Dressing

75g blue cheese, crumbled

150g 0% fat yoghurt

1 tbsp white wine vinegar

Put all the vegetables, including the tarragon but not the mustard cress, into a large salad bowl.

Make the dressing by mashing the blue cheese in a bowl until smooth, then mixing it with the yoghurt and white wine vinegar. Season well with salt and pepper.

Pour the dressing over the salad and toss thoroughly to combine. Add half the cress and toss again, then sprinkle over the rest of the cress as a garnish.

HAIRY BIKER TIP: This is good served with some cold chicken or a grilled chicken breast from the supermarket – just be sure to remove the skin to keep the calories down.

CRUNCHY ASIAN TOFU SALAD

Lots of great flavours here and the only thing you need to cook is the tofu. You need the firm, pressed tofu, not the silken kind, by the way. Lovely as a side salad or serve yourself up a double portion for a main meal.

280g block of firm, pressed tofu, diced
low-cal oil spray
150g baby leaf spinach
1 large carrot, cut into matchsticks
2 turnips, cut into matchsticks
bunch of spring onions, sliced into rounds
½ cucumber, deseeded and cut into crescents
small bunch of coriander, chopped
1 tsp black sesame seeds

Marinade

½ tsp sesame seed oil
½ tsp honey
½ tsp Szechuan peppercorns, crushed
1 tbsp soy sauce
2 garlic cloves, crushed
30g fresh root ginger, grated
sea salt and black pepper

Mix together the marinade ingredients in a bowl and season with salt and pepper. Add the tofu and turn it over gently until completely covered. Cover and leave the tofu to marinate in the fridge for an hour.

Remove the tofu from the marinade, reserving the liquid for dressing the salad. Spray a non-stick frying pan with oil, add the tofu and cook for 2 or 3 minutes on each side until well browned and crispy round the edges.

To assemble the salad, toss the spinach with the carrot, turnips, spring onions and cucumber and arrange them on a platter. Place the tofu on top, then drizzle with the marinade. Sprinkle over the coriander leaves and sesame seeds.

AVOCADO POKE BOWL

Poke (pronounced POH-keh) bowls are a Hawaiian tradition and are the ultimate in assembly job dishes. They are often made with raw fish such as tuna but we've kept ours veggie with avocado. A one-bowl wonder that counts for an amazing four of your five a day!

2 oranges

1 portion of cauliflower rice (see p.180)

2 avocados

bunch of spring onions, cut in half and shredded lengthways

½ cucumber, halved lengthways and sliced into crescents

½ Chinese cabbage, shredded

8 radishes, sliced

Dressing

2 tbsp light soy sauce

1 tsp sesame oil

1 tsp hot sauce or a pinch of chilli flakes (optional)

1 garlic clove, crushed

15g fresh root ginger, grated

juice from the oranges

sea salt and black pepper

To serve

1 tsp black or white sesame seeds

small bunch of coriander

Cut the oranges into segments. First, cut rounds from the top and bottom. Stand one of the oranges upright on a chopping board, then following its contours, carefully cut away the skin and layer of membrane. Hold the orange in your hand and cut out the segments, cutting as close to the membrane as you can. Do this over a bowl to catch the juice that will spill, then gently squeeze the membrane before you discard it. Prepare the other orange in the same way, reserving the juice for the dressing.

Next make the dressing. Add the soy sauce, sesame oil, the hot sauce or chilli flakes, if using, and the garlic and ginger to the orange juice and whisk them together. Taste for seasoning and add salt and pepper if you need to.

To assemble, divide the cauliflower rice between 4 bowls. Peel the avocados and cut the flesh into strips. Arrange the avocado, orange segments, onions, cucumber, cabbage and radishes in separate piles on top of the rice, then drizzle over the dressing. Sprinkle with the sesame seeds and garnish with the coriander. Serve immediately.

HAIRY BIKER TIP: You can also make this dish with salmon instead of avocados. Cut the salmon into 2cm cubes and then chill them until you are ready to serve. Assemble the salad as above.

Serves 4 | 267 calories per serving | Prep: 15 minutes | Cooking time: no cooking

RED SLAW AND SMOKED MACKEREL SALAD

Smoked mackerel is available everywhere and all you have to do is unwrap it and tuck in – perfect fast food. This robust, crunchy slaw is the ideal partner for the fish and makes an excellent meal.

250g red cabbage, finely shredded

100g celeriac, cut into fine matchsticks

1 large carrot, cut into fine matchsticks

1 red onion, finely sliced

1 celery stick, finely sliced

1 orange

250g smoked mackerel, skinned and torn into chunks

small bunch of dill, finely chopped

small bunch of mint, leaves only

Dressing

1 heaped tbsp half-fat crème fraiche

2 tsp wholegrain mustard

1 tsp sherry vinegar

sea salt and black pepper

Put the red cabbage, celeriac, carrot, red onion and celery into a large serving bowl. To prepare the orange, top and tail it, then cut away the skin and outer membrane. Dice the flesh, flicking out any seeds or large pieces of pith.

Mix the dressing ingredients together and season them with salt and pepper. Stir the dressing into the slaw, then add the mackerel and most of the dill and mint leaves. Stir again, then garnish with the orange and the rest of the dill and mint and serve at once.

HAIRY BIKER TIP: If you want to make this ahead of time – for example, if you want to take it to work with you in a lunchbox – you need to salt the veg to rid them of excess liquid. Put the red cabbage, celeriac, carrot, red onion and celery into a large colander and sprinkle with a teaspoon of salt, half a teaspoon of caster sugar and a teaspoon of vinegar. Mix everything together thoroughly and set the colander over a bowl or in the sink. Leave it to stand for an hour – this will help get rid of any excess liquid in the vegetables that might otherwise make the slaw soggy.

EASTERN PRAWN TACOS

We do fusion with the best of them. This recipe is East meets West and ends up in Mexico. Mega good, simple to do and a good dish for all the family to sit round the table and share.

zest of 1 lime
2 garlic cloves, grated
30g fresh root ginger, grated
a few drops of sesame oil
400g raw peeled tiger prawns
sea salt and black pepper

Sauce
2 tbsp crunchy peanut butter
juice and zest of 1 lime
1 tbsp fish sauce
½ tsp honey

To serve
¼ Chinese or white cabbage, shredded
1 red pepper, finely sliced
8 radishes, thinly sliced
½ cucumber, deseeded and cut into matchsticks
mint and coriander leaves
8 corn tortillas
lime wedges
hot sauce (such as sriracha)

First, give the prawns a quick marinade. Put the lime zest, garlic and ginger into a bowl with plenty of salt and pepper. Add the oil and prawns and toss to coat them all with the marinade, then set them aside while you prepare the rest of the dish.

For the sauce, mix the peanut butter with the lime juice, zest, fish sauce and honey. Taste for seasoning and add a little more salt if necessary.

Prepare all the vegetables and the herbs and arrange them in separate serving bowls.

Heat the tortillas in a dry frying pan one at a time – just a few seconds on each side – then wrap them in a tea towel to keep them warm.

Heat a griddle pan until very hot and cook the prawns until they are pink on both sides. Transfer to a serving dish.

To serve, just put everything on the table and let everyone spread peanut sauce on tortillas and help themselves to prawns and salad ingredients as they like. Nice with a squeeze of lime and a dash of hot sauce.

CHICKEN, SQUASH AND QUINOA SALAD

You can buy cooked quinoa or we like to cook up a big batch and keep some in the freezer – always good to have some handy for a hearty salad like this one. Then all you have to do is roast the squash and put everything together. Lunch sorted!

300g butternut squash, diced

1 tsp olive oil

½ tsp dried oregano

½ garlic bulb, cloves separated but unpeeled

150g cooked quinoa

200g baby salad leaves

200g cooked chicken, diced

1 avocado, peeled and diced

bunch of spring onions, sliced into rounds

handful of mint leaves

sea salt and black pepper

Dressing

2 tsp olive oil

zest and juice of 1 lime

1 tsp red wine vinegar

pinch of sugar

½ tsp chipotle powder (or other chilli powder)

Preheat the oven to 200°C/Fan 180°C/Gas 6. Put the squash in a roasting tin and drizzle it with the olive oil. Season well with salt and pepper, sprinkle over the oregano and add the garlic cloves. Roast the squash for about 25 minutes, until it's just tender and slightly browned around the edge. Remove the garlic and set the squash aside to cool to room temperature.

Now make the dressing. Squash the garlic flesh out of the roasted cloves and put it all in a bowl. Add the remaining dressing ingredients, season with salt and pepper, then whisk everything together.

Arrange the quinoa and salad leaves on a large platter and add the chicken, avocado, spring onions and roasted squash. Drizzle over the salad dressing, then top with the mint leaves. Serve at once.

PARMA HAM SALAD

If you've got some leftover cooked new potatoes in the fridge this is the thing to do with them – a lovely combo of crunchy potatoes, soft ham, juicy beetroot and tangy leaves. Parma ham is always cut very thin and even a small amount packs enormous flavour so you get great value for your calories. The sort of salad that's not just for summer.

low-cal oil spray
200g cooked salad potatoes, diced
100g baby leaf spinach
handful of bitter leaves such as endive
½ small onion, very finely sliced
400g cooked beetroot, cut into wedges
120g Parma ham, trimmed of fat
sea salt and black pepper

Dressing
1 tsp olive oil
2 tsp wholegrain mustard
1 tbsp sherry vinegar

Heat a frying pan and cover the base with a few squirts of oil. Add the potatoes and spritz them with oil, then season with plenty of salt. Cook the potatoes over a high heat, stirring regularly, until they are crisp and brown.

While the potatoes are cooking, arrange the spinach, then the endive or other leaves on a large platter or in individual salad bowls. Sprinkle over the onion slices, then add the wedges of beetroot. Whisk the dressing ingredients together with plenty of salt and pepper, adding a splash of water to thin it out a little. Drizzle this over the salad.

Drape the ham on top, then sprinkle over the crisp potatoes. Serve the salad immediately.

HAIR BIKER TIP: You could even make this salad with a can of baby new potatoes – a store cupboard staple.

Sometimes you feel you don't have time to deal with long lists of ingredients. For this chapter, we've come up with recipes that need no more than SIX items – not counting oil, butter, salt and pepper. Not too much shopping, not too much prep and they're all easy to put together and delicious to eat.

HALF-DOZEN WINNERS

TOMATO AND BASIL SOUP

We all love tinned tomato soup but you can make your own much more flavourful version with a couple of cans of tomatoes and some garlic, onion and herbs. This brings you a touch of Mediterranean sunshine at any time of year. A real treat.

1 onion, finely chopped

2 garlic cloves, crushed

2 x 400g cans of chopped tomatoes or rough passata

bunch of basil, roughly chopped, a few leaves reserved for garnish

100ml single cream

Heat a teaspoon of olive oil and 5 grams of butter in a saucepan. Add the onion and a pinch of salt and cook over a gentle heat until the onion is soft and translucent. Add the garlic and cook for a further minute or so, then pour in the tomatoes. Lastly add the basil and 400ml of water, then season with salt and pepper.

Bring the soup to the boil, then cover the pan, turn down the heat and leave to simmer for 15 minutes. Blitz the soup until smooth with a stick blender or in a jug blender. Stir in a lovely swirl of cream and serve with a sprinkling of shredded basil.

HAIRY BIKER TIP: You can use vegetable stock if you have some to make this soup extra tasty.

CREAMY MUSHROOM SOUP

When making soup, simple is best. You don't need loads of ingredients. Mushroom soup is a classic and our new version isn't much more trouble than opening a can but is a lot tastier and really low-cal. No need for fancy mushrooms; any kind will do.

1 onion, finely chopped

3 garlic cloves, finely chopped

2 large sprigs of tarragon, leaves only, finely chopped, plus extra to garnish

700g mushrooms, finely diced

750ml vegetable stock

Heat 10 grams of butter in a large saucepan. Add the onion and cook it gently for about 10 minutes until it's soft and translucent. Then add the garlic, tarragon and mushrooms and continue to cook until the mushrooms have given out their liquid.

Pour over the stock and season generously with salt and pepper. Bring the soup to the boil, then reduce the heat and simmer for 15 minutes.

Remove the pan from the heat and blitz the soup in a blender or with a stick blender until smooth. For extra smoothness, push the blended soup through a sieve. Reheat if necessary and serve piping hot.

HAIRY BIKER TIP: If you'd like to dress this soup up a bit and have some half-fat crème fraiche in your fridge, mix 50ml of crème fraiche with a tablespoon of chopped tarragon and season well with salt and pepper. Stir a spoonful into each serving and add a tarragon sprig.

SPAGHETTI VONGOLE

This is one of the best of all pasta recipes. Obviously, fresh clams are great but they can be pricey and we find that tinned clams make a perfectly good dish – the Italians often use them. Or try mussels instead and they are as cheap as chips.

500g clams in their shells OR a can of clams, drained

200g spaghetti

2 garlic cloves, finely chopped

½ tsp chilli flakes (or more to taste)

100ml white wine

zest of ½ lemon

If using fresh clams, give them a good wash under cold, running water and discard any that don't close when sharply tapped. Set them aside.

Bring a large pot of water to the boil and add a generous amount of salt. Add the spaghetti and cook until just al dente.

While the pasta is cooking, heat 2 teaspoons of olive oil in a large pan and add the garlic and chilli flakes. Add the fresh or canned clams, then pour over the wine. Cover the pan and leave for 2–3 minutes over a high heat, giving the pan a shake at intervals. If using fresh clams, most of them should have opened by this time. Chuck out any that haven't opened.

Drain the spaghetti and add it to the pan with the clams. Sprinkle over the lemon zest, then toss well and serve at once.

HAIRY BIKER TIP: HAIRY BIKER TIP: If you have some parsley available, finely chop some and sprinkle a little over each serving.

Serves 4 | 337 calories per serving | **Prep:** 10 minutes | **Cooking time:** about 20 minutes

SCALLOPS WITH PEA PURÉE AND CHORIZO

Scallops are expensive, but just because you're on a diet doesn't mean you can't have a treat once in a while. They're very low in calories too so a good diet food if you can afford them. Chorizo goes well with scallops and helps eke them out so you don't need so many to make a good meal.

1 leek, finely chopped

100ml whole milk

250g frozen peas, defrosted

200g cooking chorizo, peeled and diced

1 tbsp sherry vinegar

200g prepared scallops (4 or 5 small or 3 large per person)

First make the pea purée. Put the chopped leek in a small saucepan, add the milk and season with salt. Bring the milk to the boil and simmer the leek for 3–4 minutes. Reserve 2 tablespoons of the peas, and add the rest to the leeks. Simmer for another 2–3 minutes until the peas are just cooked but still fresh and green.

Tip the contents of the pan into a food processor or blender and blitz to make a purée as rough or as smooth as you like. Set the purée aside and keep it warm. Put the reserved peas in a small pan and cover them with boiling water. Heat them through gently, then drain and keep them warm.

Put the chorizo in a small frying pan and fry it briskly until browned. If there's a lot of fat in the pan, strain most of it off. Add the vinegar with a tablespoon of water and let it bubble up, then immediately remove the pan from the heat and set it aside.

Finally, cook the scallops. Heat a frying pan and spray it with oil. When the pan is hot, add the scallops and cook them for 1–2 minutes on each side until they are lightly caramelised.

Divide the pea purée between 4 plates. Add the scallops, then sprinkle over the reserved peas. Add the chorizo, then drizzle over the vinegar from the chorizo pan. Serve immediately.

HAIRY BIKER TIP: This dish looks pretty garnished with a handful of salad leaves, such as lamb's lettuce or pea shoots, if you have some.

AUBERGINES WITH HARISSA, LENTILS AND GREENS

All the big supermarkets stock ready-made harissa now. It's a spicy chilli paste from North Africa which is full of flavour and gives these aubergines a beautiful fiery red colour. This dish looks fantastic on the plate and tastes just as good. Great satisfaction value for not many calories.

2 large aubergines, halved lengthways
2–3 tbsp harissa paste
250g cooked puy lentils
200g fresh spinach
200g 0% or low-fat yogurt
2 tsp dried mint

Preheat the oven to 200°C/Fan 180°C/Gas 6. Take each aubergine half and cut a criss-cross pattern into the flesh, making sure you don't cut through the skin. Place the aubergines on a baking tray and season them generously with salt.

Thin out the harissa with a little water if it is very thick, then brush it over the aubergines. Roast the aubergines for 30–35 minutes until the flesh is soft.

Meanwhile, put the lentils in a large saucepan and add a splash of water. Add the spinach and cook until the spinach has just started to wilt down. Remove the pan from the heat and drain the lentils and spinach immediately, but not too thoroughly.

Divide the lentils and spinach between 4 plates and add the grilled aubergines. Mix the yoghurt and mint together and season with plenty of salt and pepper.

Serve with the yoghurt dressing on the side.

HAIRY BIKER TIP: You can buy packets of cooked puy lentils but if you prefer to cook your own, you will need about 100g of raw lentils.

Serves 4 | 302 calories per serving | Prep: 10 minutes | Cooking time: 15 minutes

CHILLI PRAWN PASTA

We both love chillies and there is something truly wonderful about the combo of chilli, prawns and pasta. This is so simple to make but tastes the business. The trick with pasta when you're dieting is to weigh it beforehand and stick to a small amount. It's all too easy to cook – and eat – too much.

200g linguine

3 garlic cloves, crushed

2 medium red chillies, deseeded and finely chopped

zest and juice of ½ lemon

500g raw prawns, shelled

small bunch of parsley, finely chopped

Bring a large saucepan of water to the boil. Season with a good pinch of salt and add the pasta.

Meanwhile, heat a tablespoon of olive oil in a large frying pan. Add the garlic and chillies and cook them over a medium to low heat until you can smell their aroma. Don't let the garlic take on any colour. Add the lemon zest and the prawns. Season with plenty of salt and pepper and cook the prawns for 1–2 minutes on each side.

Drain the pasta, reserving a ladleful of the cooking water. Add 3–4 tablespoons of the cooking water to the prawns, together with the lemon juice, and simmer for a couple of minutes. Add the linguine to the pan and toss everything together.

Stir in the parsley and serve at once in shallow bowls, perhaps with a crisp green salad on the side.

HAIRY BIKER TIP: We sometimes add a handful of tenderstem broccoli to the pan to cook with pasta for the last few minutes. This adds bulk but few calories.

Serves 4 | all under 350 calories per serving (see table below for exact calorie counts)
Prep: 10–15 minutes | Cooking time: up to 75 minutes

BAKED POTATOES AND FILLINGS

Baked potatoes have always been - and always will be - a go-to supper for us. And these simple but delicious fillings make the humble spud into a guilt-free meal to be proud of.

4 baking potatoes or sweet potatoes, well scrubbed and patted dry

Bacon and mushroom filling

75g smoked back bacon, trimmed of fat and diced

200g button mushrooms, thinly sliced

1 garlic clove, chopped

100g baby leaf spinach

30g low-fat quark

Broccoli and cheese filling

350g broccoli, cut into very small florets and thicker stems sliced

75g reduced-fat cheese

25g quark

1 tsp wholegrain mustard

Coronation chicken filling

(see p.22)

To make baked potatoes, preheat the oven to 200°C/Fan 180°C/Gas 6. Cut a deep cross in each potato and pierce it all over with a fork. Spray with olive oil and sprinkle with salt, then bake for 60–75 minutes. Squeeze each potato from the bottom so that the cut cross opens out. Serve with your choice of filling.

For sweet potatoes, preheat the oven to 180°C/Fan 160°C/Gas 4. Pierce each potato all over with a fork, then place the potatoes on a baking tray. Spray with olive oil and sprinkle with salt, then roast for 50–60 minutes until cooked. Split and top with filling.

For the bacon and mushroom filling, heat a teaspoon of olive oil in a frying pan. Add the bacon and cook for 2 minutes over a high heat until it starts to brown. Add the mushrooms and continue to cook over a high heat until they start to brown. Add the garlic and season well with salt and pepper. Add the spinach and stir until it has wilted – stop before it gives out lots of liquid and collapses completely. Stir in the quark and serve.

For the broccoli and cheese filling, bring a large pan of water to the boil and add salt. Boil the broccoli for 3–4 minutes or until just tender, then drain. Put the cheese in a small pan with the quark and mustard. Stir over a low heat until the cheese has melted into a sauce. Fold in the broccoli and season.

For the coronation chicken filling, see page 22.

	WHITE POTATO	SWEET POTATO
Bacon and mushroom filling	232 calories	247 calories
Broccoli and cheese filling	274 calories	289 calories
Coronation chicken filling	331 calories	346 calories

ROAST COD WITH LENTILS

Years ago we cooked sea bass with a chorizo crust on a beach in Patagonia and this dish is inspired by that. It's a touch of surf and turf if you like – cod and chorizo make good partners and this dish has a Spanish vibe to it. Quick, healthy and very good to eat.

4 x 150g skinned
cod loin fillets
1 tsp dried thyme
150g cooking
chorizo, diced
50ml Marsala or sherry
300g cherry tomatoes
250g cooked puy lentils

Preheat the oven to 200°C/Fan 180°C/Gas 6. Season the cod fillets with salt and pepper and brush them on both sides with a little olive oil. Sprinkle over the thyme, then roast the cod in the oven for 12–15 minutes until it's just cooked through. Remove the cod from the oven and set it aside.

While the cod is roasting, put the chorizo in a frying pan and cook it over a medium heat until it has browned on all sides and has rendered out plenty of oil. Strain off most of the oil, then discard it.

Turn up the heat and add the Marsala or sherry to the pan. Allow it to bubble up for a moment or so, then add the cherry tomatoes and heat until the cherry tomatoes have plumped up and almost look ready to burst. Add the lentils and stir them into the tomatoes until warm.

Pile the lentils, chorizo and cherry tomatoes on warm plates and top with the roasted cod. Serve with lots of green vegetables.

HAIRY BIKER TIP: Using ready-cooked lentils is quick and easy, but if you want to cook your own you will need about 100 grams or so.

BACON AND LENTIL SOUP

This is a lovely warming soup and a great one to put in a thermos and take out with you for a packed lunch – just right when you're on a hike. It's a proper main meal soup and ideal for batch cooking and freezing too, so double up the quantities if you like.

100g smoked back bacon, trimmed of fat, then diced

1 onion, finely chopped

1 large carrot (about 150g), finely chopped

2 celery sticks, finely diced

200g red lentils

1 large sprig of fresh thyme or 1 tsp dried thyme

Heat a teaspoon of olive oil in a large saucepan. Add the bacon and onion and fry them over a high heat until the bacon has taken on some colour. Add the carrot and celery, then turn down the heat and cook gently for 10 minutes, stirring regularly.

Stir in the red lentils and add the thyme. Pour over 1.25ml of water, season generously with salt and pepper, then bring to the boil. Turn the heat down to a simmer, partially cover the pan and cook for about half an hour, stirring regularly. By the end of this time, the lentils should have broken down and thickened the soup. Check the seasoning and adjust if necessary.

If you want a smooth soup, purée it with a stick blender or in a jug blender. Otherwise serve it piping hot in deep bowls.

HAIRY BIKER TIP: This is a Caribbean-style soup so if you fancy, add a dash of hot sauce to your bowl. We like a Scotch bonnet sauce but any kind is fine.

SAVOURY TARTLETS

We've discovered that pitta dough makes excellent tartlets and, as there is very little fat in the dough, they're not too calorific. These are good warm or at room temperature so good for lunch boxes and picnics or served with a salad or veg. We've suggested two different fillings below.

½ portion of pitta dough (see p.178)

2 eggs

100ml half-fat crème fraiche

Tomato and basil filling

16 cherry tomatoes

8 basil leaves

25g Parmesan cheese or vegetarian alternative, grated

Ham and pea filling

30g chopped ham

30g peas

8 mint leaves

(Tomato and basil filling suitable for vegetarians)

Preheat the oven to 200°C/Fan 180°C/Gas 6. Spray 8 holes in a deep muffin tray with low-cal oil. Divide the dough into 8 pieces. Roll each piece into a round and use it to line each of the oiled holes. Press the dough down into each hole – if it puffs up, pierce it with a knife to help it deflate.

Beat the eggs in a bowl, then stir in the crème fraiche. Season with salt and pepper.

Divide either the cherry tomatoes or the ham and peas, depending on what you have chosen, between the tartlet cases, then cover with the egg and crème mixture. Err on the side of caution with this and make sure you don't cover the dough completely. Put a leaf of the appropriate herb on each tartlet – basil for the tomato filling and mint for the ham and pea filling. If making the tomato version, sprinkle the tartlets with the grated Parmesan.

Bake the tartlets in the preheated oven for about 25 minutes until they are puffed up and golden brown with crisp undersides. Remove and leave them to subside, then serve warm or at room temperature.

HAIRY BIKER TIP: These freeze and reheat very well, so it's a good one to double up on – you'll need a whole portion of the pitta dough.

BREAKFAST OMELETTE BURRITOS

We used to take these on a day out fishing – we're not mean with the ingredients so they really keep you going all day. They're easy to make, then you just roll the omelettes up and off you go, breakfast in hand. It's great just as it is but also good with your favourite condiment added, such as ketchup, brown sauce or mustard. It's up to you.

2 sausages, sliced in half lengthways
4 back bacon rashers, trimmed of fat
25g plain flour
4 eggs
2 tbsp milk

Heat a griddle pan until it's very hot. Add the sausages and grill them for 4–5 minutes on the skin side. Keep pressing them down so they colour evenly and don't curl in on themselves. When the skins are nicely browned, turn the sausages over and grill the other side. Add the bacon rashers to the pan and grill them on both sides. Keep the sausages and bacon warm.

Put the flour in a bowl and season it with salt and pepper. Add one of the eggs and whisk to make a thick paste. Add the remaining eggs, one at a time, then finish with the milk to make a smooth batter.

Spray a large non-stick (25–26cm diameter) frying pan with low-cal oil. Pour in half the egg mixture and swirl it around so it coats the base of the pan in an even layer. Cook the omelette over a low to medium heat until it is just set, without letting it take on any colour on the underside. It's very important to cook the omelette slowly and gently or it will crack when you try to roll it up.

Arrange half the bacon and sausages in the middle of the omelette. If you want to add any condiments (ketchup, brown sauce or mustard) do that now. Fold the bottom of the omelette over the meat, then fold in the sides. Roll it on to a piece of foil and wrap completely, or leave the top exposed if eating at once. Repeat to make the second omelette.

SPINACH AND HAM STRUDEL

Filo is the dieter's pastry of choice and this strudel is so good. Try serving it with mashed cauliflower for a fresh take on pie and mash! Great with a pile of green veg too or a beetroot leaf salad. And if you've some filo left over, try making the apple and cinnamon strudel on page 157.

500g fresh spinach
100g ham, trimmed of fat and finely diced
150g low-fat cottage cheese
100g cherry tomatoes, diced if large
grating of nutmeg
5 large sheets of filo pastry (about 30 x 40cm)

Wash the spinach, then shake off any excess water but don't dry the leaves too thoroughly. Pile the spinach into a large pan and place it over the heat. Keep pressing down the spinach with a wooden spoon until it wilts down. When the spinach has collapsed but is still nice and fresh and green, drain it in a colander. Leave it until it's cool enough to handle, then squeeze out as much water as you can. Chop the spinach finely.

Put the spinach in a bowl with the remaining ingredients (except the filo) and season generously with salt and pepper. Stir well to combine. Preheat the oven to 200°C/Fan 180°C/Gas 6.

Lay a sheet of filo on your work surface and spritz it a couple of times with low-cal oil. Use a pastry brush to spread the oil over the pastry, then repeat until you have a pile of all 5 sheets. (If your filo sheets are smaller, just use a couple and overlap them slightly to get roughly the right size.)

Spoon the filling along the centre of the pastry, lengthways, then brush all the edges with water. Fold the shorter edges in first, then the longer sides. Turn the strudel over so the edges are on the bottom. Spray the strudel with oil, then transfer it to a baking tray.

Cook the strudel in the oven for 25–30 minutes until the pastry has lightly browned and the filling is piping hot. Serve hot or at room temperature.

CRISPY DUCK WITH PANCAKES

A quick and easy version of the Chinese favourite and seriously good. It's something you might never have thought of making but this is well worth a shot. We've suggested using bought pancakes here for speed but make your own if you have time – there's a recipe on page 179.

3 duck breasts, skinned

30g fresh root ginger, finely grated

1 bunch of spring onions, finely shredded lengthways

½ cucumber, deseeded and cut into thin strips

8 small Chinese pancakes

40g hoisin sauce (1 tsp per pancake)

Put the duck breasts in a saucepan and cover them with water. Add salt, then bring the water to the boil. Turn down the heat to a simmer, and poach the breasts for about 10 minutes until the meat is cooked through and tender. Remove the breasts from the liquid, place them on a chopping board and shred the meat as finely as you can.

Heat 2 teaspoons of vegetable oil in a wok. When the air above the oil has started to shimmer, the oil will be hot enough to add the duck. Fry the meat briskly for 3–4 minutes, until it is crisping up nicely round the edges, then add the ginger. Season generously with salt and pepper and continue to stir-fry until the duck is crisp. Transfer it to a warmed serving plate.

Arrange the spring onions and cucumber on a serving dish and heat the pancakes according to the packet instructions.

To eat, spread the pancakes with hoisin sauce, add duck, spring onions and cucumber, then roll up and enjoy.

HAIRY BIKER TIP: For a change, you could also serve the duck with lots of stir-fried veg instead of the pancakes. Makes a great supper.

Serves 4 | 273 calories per serving | **Prep:** 10 minutes | **Cooking time:** 30–35 minutes

POACHED CHICKEN AND TARRAGON SAUCE

This is the dieter's version of a French classic without the hassle. Gentle poaching is a very simple way to cook chicken breasts and gives you lovely tender meat. Then you use the poaching liquid to make a tasty sauce and serve it all up with some new potatoes and green vegetables.

4 skinless chicken breasts
bunch of tarragon
3 garlic cloves, sliced
pared zest and juice
of ½ lemon
400g baby new potatoes
100ml half-fat crème
fraiche

Season the chicken breasts with salt and white pepper and put them in a lidded frying pan. They should fit quite snugly. Add a large tarragon sprig, the sliced garlic and the lemon zest, then pour over just enough water to cover the chicken breasts.

Bring the water to the boil, then turn down the heat so it is just below simmering point. Leave the chicken to cook very gently for 7 minutes, then check for doneness. Pierce a skewer into the thickest part – any juices should run clear and the skewer should feel too hot to touch. Cook for longer if necessary.

Meanwhile, bring a large saucepan of water to the boil and add salt. Add the new potatoes and simmer them for about 15 minutes or so until cooked. Drain them and keep them warm.

Remove the chicken from poaching liquid and set it aside to keep warm. Place the pan over the heat again and cook to reduce the liquid to about 200ml. Strain it and discard the garlic and tarragon, then stir in the crème fraiche. Finely chop the remaining tarragon and stir it into the sauce. Taste and add as much of the lemon juice as you think necessary, a teaspoon at a time. Serve the chicken breasts and potatoes with the sauce spooned over or in a separate jug.

HAIRY BIKER TIP: Green beans go well with this. To save using another pan, add the beans to the potatoes for the last 3 or 4 minutes of the cooking time. Remove the beans with tongs, then drain the potatoes.

GARLIC CHICKEN WITH BEANS, KALE AND CHERRY TOMATOES

Slicing chicken breasts in half like this creates two nice thin pieces from each breast so they cook quickly without getting tough. The rest is easy and makes a good simple meal.

4 chicken breasts, skinned

4 garlic cloves, crushed

200g kale, shredded

400g can of cannellini beans, drained and rinsed

300g cherry tomatoes, halved

1 tbsp sherry vinegar

First prepare the chicken. Place each breast on a work surface with the top side facing up. Put one hand on the chicken breast, then slice through into the side of the breast, continuing to slice horizontally until you have cut all the way through.

Put a tablespoon of olive oil and the crushed garlic in a bowl. Season the chicken pieces well with salt and pepper, then add them to the bowl. Rub the chicken with the garlic and olive oil until it's all thoroughly coated, then if you have time, leave them to marinate for half an hour.

When you are ready to cook the chicken, heat a large griddle pan until it is too hot to hold your hand over, then turn the heat down to medium. Cook the chicken breasts for 3–4 minutes on each side until they have char lines and are completely cooked through. You may need to do this in a couple of batches – if so keep the first batch warm while you cook the second batch.

Meanwhile, bring a large pan of water to the boil and add plenty of salt. Cook the kale for 3 minutes until almost cooked, then add the beans to heat through for a minute. Drain well.

To assemble, divide the kale and beans between 4 plates. Cut the chicken breasts diagonally into strips and add them to the plates. Sprinkle over the cherry tomatoes, then drizzle over the sherry vinegar and serve immediately.

LIVER AND ONIONS

Don't be put off by memories of school dinners. Offal is a great source of protein so give it a go. We've always been big fans of liver and while we love it with bacon, this version of the Italian way of cooking liver is another favourite. And it still goes well with some fluffy mash.

3 onions, thinly sliced

500g calf or lamb's liver, thinly sliced into strips

100ml Marsala or sherry

1 tsp dried sage or a few fresh sage leaves, shredded

500g potatoes, diced

50ml half-fat crème fraiche

Heat a teaspoon of olive oil with 15 grams of butter in a large, heavy-based frying pan. When the butter has melted and is foaming, add the onions. Cook the onions over a low heat, stirring regularly, until they are very soft and are a light golden brown – they will start sticking together when they are almost ready. If they are cooking too quickly, add a splash of water to the frying pan.

Remove the onions from the pan and keep them warm. Turn the heat up and add a couple more teaspoons of oil. Season the strips of liver with salt and pepper and add them to the pan. Sear them quickly – they should only need a minute or so on each side to be pink in the middle. If you prefer your liver cooked through, cook it for a little longer.

Put the onions back in the pan and add the Marsala or sherry, 50ml of water and the sage leaves. Make sure you scrape up any brown bits from the base of the pan, then simmer for a few minutes until the sauce is well reduced and sticky.

Meanwhile, put the potatoes in a saucepan, cover them with cold water and add salt. Bring the water to the boil, partially cover the pan and cook for 12–15 minutes until tender. Drain the potatoes thoroughly and either mash them or put them through a ricer. Whip in the crème fraiche.

Serve the liver and onions with the mash and some green veg.

We've always loved one-pot dishes and from the feedback we get, we know you do too. You don't end up with a sinkful of pots and pans and somehow cooking everything together makes it all taste even more delicious. Here are some of our favourites — from soups and risottos to tray bakes and hotpots.

ONE-POT WONDERS

BEETROOT SOUP

We cooked beetroot soup – borscht – in Latvia and it's just as tasty in Luton. This is our quick, simple version and it's a good, economical and robust dish. We like to use beef stock but you can use veg stock instead if you prefer to make a great vegetarian soup.

2 tsp olive oil or 10g butter

1 large carrot, diced

1 onion, diced

2 celery sticks, diced

2 floury potatoes (about 300g), diced

500g cooked beetroot, diced

1 litre beef stock *

½ small green cabbage, shredded

2 garlic cloves, finely sliced or chopped

sea salt and black pepper

To serve

small bunch of dill, finely chopped

4 dessertspoons of half-fat crème fraiche or soured cream

(*or vegetable stock for the veggie option)

Heat the oil or butter in a large saucepan. Add the diced carrot, onion, celery, potatoes and 400g of the beetroot. Cook for several minutes until everything is starting to soften and brown around the edges, then add the stock. Season with salt and pepper, then simmer for 10 minutes.

Add the cabbage and garlic, and cook for a further 15 minutes. Then add the remaining beetroot and continue to cook until it is heated through.

Serve the soup garnished with a sprinkling of chopped dill and spoonfuls of crème fraiche or soured cream.

HAIRY BIKER TIP: For a really substantial soup, add a few slices of shredded roast beef at the last minute – especially if you've made the roast beef on page 140 and have some leftovers.

CAULIFLOWER CHEESE SOUP

Macaroni cheese might be off the menu for dieters but this cauli cheese soup ticks all the boxes and warms the cockles of your heart. And it counts for two of your five a day!

5g butter

1 onion, finely chopped

1 potato (about 150g), diced

1 small cauliflower (500–600g), broken into florets

750ml vegetable stock

100g reduced-fat vegetarian Cheddar, grated

250ml whole milk

50g half-fat crème fraiche

1 tbsp wholegrain mustard

a few chives, finely chopped

sea salt and black pepper

Melt the butter in a large saucepan and add the chopped onion. Cook over a medium heat for several minutes, stirring regularly, until the onion has started to caramelise, then add the potato and cauliflower. Pour over the vegetable stock and season with salt and pepper.

Bring the soup to the boil, then turn the heat down and partially cover the pan. Simmer until the potato and cauliflower are both tender – this will take about 10 minutes.

Stir in the cheese until it has melted. Using a hand-held stick blender or jug blender, blitz the soup until it's very smooth.

Add the milk and crème fraiche to the soup, then reheat it gently. Ladle the soup into bowls and add a dollop of wholegrain mustard and some chopped chives to each serving.

HAIRY BIKER TIP: To make this soup even cheesier, replace half the Cheddar with grated Parmesan (or vegetarian equivalent) for extra flavour.

BAKED VEGETABLE RISOTTO

We're big fans of risotto but who wants to stand at the stove stirring for half an hour? In this version you get the cooking started on the hob, then pop the risotto in the oven to take care of itself while you get on with something else – perhaps some exercise, so you can have an extra helping!

1 tsp olive oil

15g butter

1 onion, finely chopped

200g Swiss chard, stems and leaves separated and shredded

zest of 1 lemon

2 garlic cloves, finely chopped

200g risotto rice, rinsed

1 large courgette, diced

200g peas

100ml white wine

600ml vegetable stock

25g Parmesan cheese or vegetarian alternative, grated

small bunch of basil, shredded

sea salt and black pepper

Preheat the oven to 150°C/Fan 130°C/Gas 2.

Heat the olive oil and butter in a large flameproof casserole dish. When the butter is foaming, add the onion and cook it over a low heat until it's translucent. Add the chard stems, lemon zest and garlic, then continue to cook for a further 5 minutes.

Add the rice, courgette, peas and chard leaves, then stir to combine. Pour in the wine and bring it to the boil, then add the stock and bring it back to the boil. Season with salt and pepper.

Transfer the casserole dish to the oven and bake the risotto, uncovered, for 20 minutes. Remove the dish from the oven and stir, then put it back in the oven for a further 15 minutes. Remove and stir in the Parmesan cheese and basil, then serve the risotto immediately.

PESTO-STUFFED MUSHROOMS

Someone used to say that life is too short to stuff a mushroom, but we disagree when it comes to these! Doesn't take too long and they make a really tasty dish with the butter beans and spinach. You could buy the pesto, but the recipe below has much less oil than usual, so is lower in calories.

4 large field or Portobello mushrooms, wiped clean

25g panko breadcrumbs

1 large courgette, sliced diagonally

low-cal oil spray

1 tbsp tomato purée

1 tsp dried oregano

400g can of butter beans, drained

100g spinach, washed

Pesto

50g fresh basil, leaves only

30g Parmesan cheese or vegetarian alternative, grated

25g pine nuts

zest and juice of 1 lemon

1 tbsp olive oil

sea salt and black pepper

Preheat the oven to 200°C/Fan 180°C/Gas 6.

To make the pesto, put all the ingredients in a small food processor and season with salt and pepper. Blitz to make a coarse paste, stopping to push down the ingredients in the bowl and adding a little water if necessary.

Place the mushrooms in a roasting tin, undersides facing up. Spread a tablespoon of pesto over each mushroom and top with some breadcrumbs. Add the courgette slices in between the mushrooms and spray them with oil. Put the tin in the oven and roast the mushrooms for 10 minutes.

Mix the tomato purée and oregano with 100ml of water in a bowl and stir in the butter beans. Take the tin out of the oven and add the butter bean mixture, taking care that the liquid doesn't go over the mushrooms – it's fine for it to cover the courgettes. Cook for a further 20 minutes.

Remove the tin from the oven. Arrange the spinach over 4 plates and top with the stuffed mushrooms, courgettes and butter beans.

Serves 4 | 346 calories per serving | **Prep:** 15 minutes | **Cooking time:** 15–20 minutes

THAI PRAWN AND VEGETABLE CURRY

This is so quick to prepare and makes a beautifully fragrant and satisfying meal. Great just as it is or served with some cauliflower rice (see page 180) or with ordinary rice for non-dieters.

2 tbsp red curry paste (or more to taste)

400ml can of reduced-fat coconut milk

200ml chicken or vegetable stock

juice and zest of 1 lime

1 tbsp fish sauce

1 red pepper, cut into strips

200g baby corn

150g green beans

200g button mushrooms

200g greens (such as pak choi), roughly chopped

400g raw peeled prawns

1 large carrot, spiralised or cut into thin strips

1 large courgette, spiralised or cut into strips

To serve

bunch of coriander, chopped

lime wedges

Put the curry paste in a large saucepan and pour in the coconut milk. Whisk to combine, then place the pan on the heat and add the stock, lime juice and zest and the fish sauce. Bring to the boil, then turn the heat down to a simmer.

Add the red pepper, baby corn, green beans, mushrooms and greens and simmer for 6–7 minutes, until the vegetables are just cooked through.

Arrange the prawns in a single layer on top of the broth. Put the carrot on top, followed by the courgette. Cover the pan and leave everything to steam for 5 minutes.

Serve in large bowls, spooning out the carrot and courgette first. Sprinkle with plenty of chopped coriander and serve with lime wedges to squeeze over.

HAIRY BIKER TIP: You could make this with chunks of white fish instead of prawns. Just leave them to steam in the same way as above.

MUSSELS WITH BACON AND CIDER

Mussels are some of the cheapest things on the fish counter and are among the tastiest too, so let's eat them more often. They partner really well with bacon and this is a great way to enjoy them. With the potatoes and vegetables, this is a proper main event dish, not a starter.

1 bag of mussels
(about 1kg)
300ml cider
100g lean back bacon,
trimmed of fat and diced
1 leek, sliced into rounds
300g new potatoes, sliced
1 tsp Dijon mustard
250g spring greens or
green cabbage, roughly
chopped
100ml single cream
(optional)
sea salt and black pepper

Prepare the mussels. Wash them thoroughly under cold water, pulling off the beards and discarding any that don't close when you give them a sharp tap. Rinse the mussels a couple of times to get rid of any grit.

Pour the cider into a large saucepan and add 200ml of water. Add the bacon, leek and new potatoes, season with salt and pepper, then bring to the boil. Turn down the heat, put a lid on the pan and leave to simmer for about 15 minutes or until the potatoes are just tender.

Stir in the mustard, then add the spring greens or cabbage. Continue to cook for another 5–6 minutes until the leaves are wilted down and just cooked through – they should still look nice and bright and green.

Add the mussels to the pan, cover and leave them to cook for 2–3 minutes. When the mussels are fully open, stir in the cream, if using.

Remove the pan from the heat and serve the mussels and vegetables immediately in deep bowls. Discard any mussels that haven't opened.

HAIRY BIKER TIP: We like the cream in this but if you don't want to include it, you're looking at only 243 calories per serving.

SALMON AND BROCCOLI TRAY BAKE

The beauty of a tray bake is that all the flavours work together and you get lots of lovely little caramelised bits to enjoy. Oily fish is incredibly good for us and a tray bake is a nice easy way of cooking it. The honey and vinegar in this recipe add little touches of sweetness and tartness, which work perfectly with the salmon. This is a really good balanced meal.

½ tsp honey

2 tsp balsamic vinegar

1 garlic clove, crushed

4 x 150g salmon fillets, skinned

1 large head of broccoli, broken into florets

200g baby salad potatoes, halved lengthways

1 red pepper, thickly sliced

1 red onion, sliced into thin wedges

low-cal oil spray (preferably olive)

250g white cup mushrooms, left whole

small bunch of basil leaves

sea salt and black pepper

Preheat the oven to 200°C/Fan 180°C/Gas 6. To make the marinade for the salmon, mix the honey, balsamic vinegar and garlic in a bowl and season with salt and pepper. Brush this mixture over both sides of the salmon and leave it to marinate while you start cooking the vegetables.

Wash the broccoli and without brushing off too much of the water and put it in a roasting tin. Add the potatoes, red pepper and onion, then spritz with some oil. Roast the vegetables in the oven for 20 minutes.

Add the salmon and mushrooms to the tin and roast for another 12 minutes until the salmon is just cooked through. Remove the tin from the oven and add a few basil leaves, then serve the tray bake immediately.

MEDITERRANEAN FISH CASSEROLE

Cooking fish in an aromatic broth in this way is so easy – you can't go wrong. The dish has a really lovely fresh, zingy flavour and brings a touch of Mediterranean sunshine to your table at any time of year. It's awesomely low in calories too so you can afford to serve plenty of extra veg.

2 tsp olive oil

1 large fennel bulb, trimmed and sliced into 8 wedges

1 red pepper, cut into strips

300g baby new potatoes, halved if large

2 garlic cloves, finely chopped

1 strip of pared orange zest

sprig of thyme

150ml white wine

400ml fish or vegetable stock

200g fresh tomatoes, peeled and chopped (or canned equivalent)

4 x 150g white fish fillets, skinned and left whole

sea salt and black pepper

Heat the olive oil in a large flameproof casserole dish. Add the fennel wedges and sear them on both sides until nicely caramelised. Add the red pepper, potatoes and garlic and cook for 3–4 minutes.

Add the orange zest, thyme, white wine and stock. Season with salt and pepper, then bring everything to the boil. Turn down the heat, cover the casserole dish with a lid and leave to simmer for about 10 minutes. Add the tomatoes and continue to cook for another 10 minutes or until the vegetables are tender.

Season the fish fillets with salt and pepper, then place them on top of the vegetables. Cover the dish and leave the fish to steam for 7–8 minutes. Serve in wide, shallow bowls.

CHICKEN TRAY BAKE WITH FENNEL, PEAS AND NEW POTATOES

A chicken tray bake is a trusty favourite for both of us and this is our latest version. We reckon it will be a go-to supper in households around the country. There are lots of lovely flavours and a good range of textures thanks to the different vegetables.

1 large or 2 small fennel bulbs, trimmed and sliced into 8 wedges

200g baby new potatoes, sliced lengthways

8 skinless, boneless chicken thigh fillets, trimmed of any fat

100ml white wine

juice and zest of 1 lemon

1 tsp dried thyme

300g peas

2 little gem lettuces, halved lengthways

low-cal oil spray (preferably olive)

sea salt and black pepper

Preheat the oven to 200°C/Fan 180°C/Gas 6. Arrange the fennel and potatoes in a large roasting tin, then drape the chicken thighs on top, partially covering the fennel. Pour over the white wine and lemon juice, then sprinkle on the zest and thyme. Season generously with salt and pepper.

Cover the roasting tin with foil and put it in the oven for 30 minutes. Then remove the tin from the oven, take off the foil and pour the peas in around the chicken. Uncover the fennel and potatoes as you go – you want them to crisp up, not to be smothered in peas. Tuck in the little gems around the veg.

Spritz with oil, then bake for another 30–35 minutes, uncovered, until the potatoes and fennel are tender and the potatoes have crisped up a bit around the edges.

DUCK AND NOODLE BROTH

It wasn't just the Marx Brothers who loved duck soup and with ours you can have noodles too!
There are quite a few ingredients here we know, but the dish couldn't be easier to prepare.
All you have to do is put everything in a pan and you'll have a real taste treat in no time.

1.5 litres chicken stock

3 garlic cloves, sliced

25g fresh root
ginger, sliced

2 tbsp soy sauce

1 red pepper, thinly sliced

1 large carrot, sliced
into matchsticks

200g broccoli
florets, sliced

½ Chinese cabbage or pak
choi, thickly shredded

200g shiitake
mushrooms, sliced

2 duck breasts, skinned
and thinly sliced

300g cooked egg noodles

sea salt and black pepper

Garnish

bunch of spring onions,
sliced diagonally

1 red chilli, finely sliced

a few drops of sesame oil

First put the stock in a large saucepan. Bring it to the boil and add the garlic, ginger and soy. Simmer for 5 minutes, then taste and season with salt and pepper.

Add all the vegetables and simmer for a few minutes until they are just tender. Add the sliced duck breasts, then put the noodles on top and cover the pan so the noodles heat through while the duck cooks. Remove the pan from the heat after a minute or so.

Divide the noodles between 4 deep bowls and ladle over the broth, vegetables and duck. Serve garnished with spring onions, chilli and sesame oil – you can add a little extra soy sauce too if you like.

SAUSAGE CASSEROLE

Everyone loves sausages and beans and here they are cooked up with lots of good veg to
make a substantial meal to delight the heart of every dieter. Get stuck in!

1 tsp olive oil

8 pork sausages

1 large onion, sliced
into thin wedges

2 carrots, thickly sliced
diagonally

3 celery sticks, thickly
sliced diagonally

3 garlic cloves, finely
chopped

1 tsp dried thyme

150ml red wine

200ml chicken stock

400g can of tomatoes

400g can of beans
(cannellini, haricot
or flageolet)

handful of parsley leaves

sea salt and black pepper

Heat the oil in a large flameproof casserole dish. Add the
sausages and fry briskly, turning them regularly until they're
well browned. Remove the sausages from the dish and set
them aside, then add the onion, carrots and celery. Cook the
vegetables over a medium heat for about 10 minutes until they
are starting to caramelise around the edges.

Add the garlic and thyme and continue to cook for 2–3 minutes.
Put the sausages back in the dish, then pour over the red wine.
Bring to the boil and reduce the wine by half, then pour in the
stock. Season with salt and pepper. Bring everything back to
the boil, then cover the dish with a lid and turn down the heat.
Simmer for 10 minutes or until the vegetables are tender.

Add the tomatoes and beans, then continue to simmer, covered,
for 20 minutes. Remove the lid and cook uncovered for another
10 minutes until the sauce has reduced. Serve with a generous
sprinkling of parsley.

*HAIRY BIKER TIP: Be sure to get sausages with a high meat content, as
they contain more protein and less fat. We like peppery Cumberland
sausages and herby Lincolnshire or why not try a Toulouse?*

HOTDOG HOTPOT

Wow – this is what we call a good supper. Frankfurters might have a slightly dodgy image but they are really nice and the ones in a jar are a great store cupboard item. This hotpot contains everything you need for hearty warming meal. There's plenty of flavour and fun and very little washing up.

1 tsp olive oil

1 onion, cut into wedges

360g jumbo frankfurters, cut into 4cm lengths

400g floury potatoes, washed but unpeeled and cut into 3cm chunks

1 eating apple, peeled and cut into 8 wedges

1 tbsp dried sage

200ml cider

200ml chicken, beef or vegetable stock

300g savoy cabbage (about ½ medium-sized), cut into 8 wedges

sea salt and black pepper

Heat the olive oil in a large flameproof casserole dish. Add the onion and frankfurters and cook them gently over a high heat until the frankfurters are lightly browned all over.

Cut the potatoes into 3cm chunks and add them to the dish with the apple wedges and sage, then season with salt and pepper. Pour over the cider and bring it to the boil. Cook until the cider has reduced by half, then add the stock – it should just cover the potatoes.

Put the wedges of savoy cabbage on top so they will steam, then bring the liquid back to the boil. Turn down the heat and cover the dish, then leave the hotpot to cook for 45 minutes.

By this point the potatoes should have started to break down and thicken the stock. Leave the hotpot to simmer uncovered for a further 15 minutes to concentrate the cooking liquid, then serve it piping hot.

Serves 4 | 168 calories per serving
Prep: 15 minutes, plus marinating | Cooking time: about 12 minutes

CHOP SUEY

People say that chop suey – a takeaway regular – was actually created in America, not China, but all we know is that it is a great dish to cook when you want something mega delicious in a hurry. It gives you that nice Chinese food hit and as it's bulked out with bean sprouts it's low in calories.

Pork
1 egg white
2 tsp cornflour
2 tsp rice wine or mirin
250g pork steak, cut into slim strips

Stir-fry
2 tsp vegetable oil
bunch of spring onions, sliced into rounds
1 red pepper, cut into fine strips
200g broccoli florets, sliced
2 garlic cloves, finely chopped
30g fresh root ginger, finely chopped
1 red chilli, sliced into thin rounds
2 tbsp soy sauce
1 tbsp mirin or rice wine
150g bean sprouts

To serve
a few drops of sesame oil
handful of chopped coriander

First prepare the pork. Whisk the egg white in a bowl until smooth. Mix the cornflour with the rice wine or mirin, whisk this into the egg white, then add the pork. Stir to coat all the pieces, then cover and leave to marinate for at least half an hour – or overnight if you like.

Heat a teaspoon of the oil in a wok. When the air above the oil is shimmering, add the pork and cook it for 2–3 minutes. Remove the pork from the wok with a slotted spoon and set it aside.

Add the remaining oil. When the air is shimmering again, add the spring onions, red pepper and broccoli. Cook them for 3–4 minutes, then add the garlic, ginger and chilli. Continue to cook for another couple of minutes, then pour in the soy sauce and the mirin.

Return the pork to the wok with the bean sprouts and stir-fry for another minute or until everything is heated through. Serve sprinkled with a little sesame oil and coriander.

HAIRY BIKER TIP: The first part of this recipe uses a technique called velveting, which is popular in Chinese cooking. Marinating the meat in egg white and cornflour like this helps prevent it becoming dry and overcooked when stir-fried.

BRAISED LAMB AND BARLEY

Barley and lamb go brilliantly together and this is a wonderful dish that's somewhere between a thick Scotch broth and a barley risotto. It freezes well too so you can make plenty and put some in the freezer to enjoy another day. Counts for three of your five a day too.

500g lean lamb (leg works best), trimmed of fat
1 tsp olive oil
1 onion, chopped
2 celery sticks, diced
1 large carrot, diced
2 garlic cloves, finely chopped
25g red lentils
100g barley
a few sprigs of rosemary or 2 tsp dried rosemary
700ml lamb or veal stock
2 leeks, cut into rounds
200g broad beans (frozen are fine)
200g greens (kale, spring greens, chard or half a small savoy cabbage)
squeeze of lemon juice
sea salt and black pepper

Cut the lamb into fairly small dice and set it aside.

Heat the olive oil in a large flameproof casserole dish or a saucepan. Add the onion, celery and carrot and sauté them over a medium heat until they're starting to soften around the edges.

Add the garlic and lamb, then turn up the heat and cook briskly until the lamb has lightly browned. Add the lentils, barley and rosemary, stir to combine, then pour over the stock. Season well with salt and pepper, then put the leek rounds on the top.

Bring to the boil, then turn the heat down to a low simmer and cover the dish or pan with a lid. Leave to cook for an hour, by which time the lamb should be close to tender and the barley plump but still with a nice little bite to it. Check the liquid level after half an hour and add a little more stock or water if necessary.

Stir in the broad beans and arrange the greens on top to steam. Cook for a further 20 minutes or until the greens have cooked through. Taste for seasoning and add a squeeze of lemon juice. Serve immediately.

We love to make life easier and we find that once you're in the kitchen you might as well cook up a storm and save on time, fuel and money. It's a lovely feeling to know you've got plenty in the freezer for days when you're in a rush. We've also added some great recipes for using up leftovers from a Sunday roast beef or chicken. Waste not, want not!

BATCH COOKING

Serves 4 | 290 calories per serving | **Prep:** 15 minutes | **Cooking time:** 25 minutes

VEGETARIAN PASTA

This pasta dish freezes and reheats well so it's a good idea to make a big batch and store some away in the freezer for another day. You can double up the quantities if you like. It's perfect for the unexpected vegetarian guest – they'll be well impressed when you produce this one.

2 tsp olive oil

1 onion, finely chopped

1 celery stick, finely chopped

2 garlic cloves, finely chopped

1 large courgette, diced

1 tsp dried rosemary, or a sprig of fresh, finely chopped

zest of ½ lemon

200g cavolo nero, shredded

150g broad beans (frozen are fine)

250ml vegetable stock

2 medium tomatoes, peeled and finely chopped

200g short pasta, such as farfalle

sea salt and black pepper

To serve

grated Parmesan cheese or vegetarian alternative (5g per serving)

Heat the olive oil in a saucepan, add the onion and celery, then sauté them over a medium heat until they're soft and translucent. Add the garlic and courgette and cook for another couple of minutes.

Sprinkle over the rosemary and lemon zest, then add the cavolo nero and broad beans. Pour over the stock, add the tomatoes, then simmer, uncovered, until the liquid has reduced by two-thirds and the vegetables are tender. Season with salt and pepper.

Meanwhile, bring a large saucepan of water to the boil and add salt. Add the pasta and cook it until just al dente – cooked but with a little bite to it.

Drain the pasta and toss it with the sauce to combine. Serve with a little grated cheese.

HAIRY BIKER TIP: If you freeze this dish, let it defrost naturally, then put it in a saucepan with a splash of water. Cover the pan and warm the pasta through over a low heat.

CHICKPEA CURRY

A really tasty veggie dish, this freezes well so it's good to make a big batch. It's also a great one to prepare ahead, as it tastes even better the next day. Tamarind paste is available in supermarkets and goes beautifully with coconut milk and the seeds, if you're using them, to give this curry a fab flavour. It's packed with veg so counts for four of your five a day!

1 tbsp vegetable or coconut oil

1 tsp mustard seeds (optional)

1 tsp nigella seeds (optional)

2 red onions, cut into wedges

2 red peppers, cut into strips

200g butternut squash, diced

3 garlic cloves, finely chopped

30g fresh root ginger, grated

1 tbsp medium curry powder

3 tbsp tamarind paste (not concentrate)

400ml reduced-fat coconut milk

400g kale, spring greens or green cabbage, shredded

2 x 400g cans of chickpeas, drained

sea salt and black pepper

Heat the oil in a large saucepan or a flameproof casserole dish. Add the seeds, if using, and fry them until they splutter. Add the onions and peppers and sauté them over a high heat for 5 minutes, stirring regularly. You want to start the cooking process but keep some texture in the veg.

Add the butternut squash, garlic, ginger and curry powder. Stir for a minute or so, then add the tamarind paste, coconut milk and 100ml of water. Season with salt and pepper. Bring to the boil, then stir in the greens.

Turn down the heat, cover the pan or dish and simmer for 15 minutes until the squash and greens are tender. Stir in the chickpeas and simmer for a further 5 minutes.

Serve the curry on its own or with a portion of steamed rice.

HAIRY BIKER TIP: If you want to cook your own chickpeas you need about 250 grams dried raw weight to make 500 grams (or slightly more) cooked.

CRISPY PANCAKES

We had a recipe for these favourites from our childhood in our *Meat Feasts* cookbook but here is a lower-calorie veggie version. The pancakes can be frozen before cooking so just assemble them, open freeze them on a baking tray, then wrap them well and put in a container or a freezer bag. Quark is a low-fat soft cheese and is available in supermarkets.

Pancakes
80g plain flour
pinch of salt
1 egg
200ml milk
low-cal oil spray

Filling
1 tsp olive oil
5g butter
1 onion, finely chopped
500g mushrooms, diced
2 garlic cloves, crushed
a few sprigs of tarragon, finely chopped
50ml white wine
175g quark
1 tbsp half-fat crème fraiche
sea salt and black pepper

To assemble
75g 0% fat Greek yoghurt
100g panko breadcrumbs

First make the pancakes. Put the flour in a bowl with a pinch of salt. Whisk to remove any lumps, then add the egg. Gradually work the egg into the flour until you have a very stiff paste, then drizzle in the milk, whisking to make a smooth, lump-free batter. Alternatively, put all the ingredients into a food processor and pulse until you have a smooth batter. Leave the batter to rest for half an hour.

Take a small frying pan – 14–16cm in diameter – and spritz the base with oil. Add a small ladleful of batter and swirl it around the pan until the base is evenly covered. Cook until the batter has set on the underside, then flip the pancake over to cook the other side. Repeat to make 8 pancakes, spraying the pan with oil in between each one. Leave them to cool.

To make the filling, heat the olive oil and butter in a frying pan. Add the onion and sauté it over a medium heat until soft. Turn up the heat and add the mushrooms, cooking and stirring until they are done. Some liquid may come out of the mushrooms as they shrink down so continue to cook until this has evaporated. Add the garlic and stir for a couple more minutes, then add the tarragon and plenty of salt and pepper.

Pour over the wine and leave it to bubble for a minute, then add the quark, stirring until it has softened and combined with the mushrooms. Add the crème fraiche and stir again – the texture should be similar to that of a fairly thick béchamel sauce. Set the filling aside to cool down.

To assemble the pancakes, put 2 heaped tablespoons of the filling on one side of each pancake, making sure you leave a generous border. Wet the edges of the pancake with water, then fold them over and press to seal as firmly as you can.

Put the yoghurt and breadcrumbs on separate plates. Brush each pancake with yoghurt, making sure each is coated in a thin, even layer on both sides. Dip each pancake in the breadcrumbs. The pancakes can be frozen at this stage. Otherwise, preheat the oven to 200°C/Fan 180°C/Gas 6.

To cook, put the pancakes on a couple of baking trays and spritz them with low-cal oil. Bake them in the preheated oven for 15–20 minutes until they are a crisp golden brown.

HAIRY BIKER TIP: You could also fill the pancakes with beef ragu (see page 142) or substitute some cooked chicken for half the mushrooms.

WHOLE POACHED CHICKEN WITH GREMOLATA

Poaching is a brilliant way to cook a chicken. It's easy to do, gives you tender, moist meat and it's lower in calories than usual because you remove the skin. And be sure to make chicken soup (page 132) with the leftovers. Gremolata is a simple lemon, parsley and garlic sauce.

1 x 1.5–2kg chicken

1 fennel bulb, trimmed and cut into wedges

2 large carrots, cut into chunks

200g waxy potatoes, halved or quartered

2 garlic cloves, chopped

sprig of tarragon

sprig of parsley

2 bay leaves

strip of pared lemon zest

up to 750ml chicken stock or water

2 courgettes, cut into thick diagonal slices

sea salt and black pepper

Gremolata

zest of 1 lemon

small bunch of parsley, finely chopped

1 garlic clove, finely chopped

(Chicken meat, carcass and broth can all be frozen separately.)

First, cut off the chicken wings and save them for stock or roast them for a treat. Next, pull the skin off the chicken. Simply push your hand in between the skin and flesh and work it away, cutting wherever necessary. Remove any large pieces of fat as you go – there will be some around the main cavity opening. Wash your hands thoroughly after handling the raw chicken.

Put the chicken in a flameproof casserole dish – it should be a fairly snug fit. Tuck the fennel, carrots, potatoes and garlic around the chicken and add the herbs and lemon zest. Add just enough stock, or water, to cover the thickest part of the leg – the top of the breasts and legs will stick up out of the liquid. Bring to the boil, then turn down the heat and season with salt and pepper. Cover and simmer the chicken for 45 minutes.

Add the courgettes and simmer for a further 15 minutes. Remove the pan from the heat and leave the chicken to stand for another 15 minutes. Check for doneness – the juices in the thickest part of the leg should run clear when pierced.

Remove the chicken from the broth and put it on a warmed serving dish. Arrange the vegetables around it, then cover everything with foil to keep warm. Bring the broth to a fierce boil and reduce it by a third. Mix the gremolata ingredients together and season with salt. Spoon a little of the reduced broth over the chicken and vegetables, reserving the rest for soup. Serve the chicken with the gremolata on the side for sprinkling.

CHUNKY CHICKEN SOUP

Make this fab soup with any leftovers from your poached chicken. It's so nourishing and the spices and ginger give it a lovely warming flavour. It feels good for you and it tastes epic.

2 tsp olive oil

2 red onions, cut into wedges

2 large carrots, cut into chunks

40g basmati rice, rinsed

3 garlic cloves, finely chopped

30g fresh root ginger, finely chopped

¼ tsp turmeric (optional)

¼ tsp cinnamon (optional)

1 litre chicken stock

1 large sweet potato, cut into chunks

200g chard or kale, shredded

200g leftover chicken, pulled into chunks

squeeze of lemon juice

sea salt and black pepper

Heat the olive oil in a large saucepan and add the onions and carrots. Sauté them over a high heat for a few minutes until they're starting to take on some colour, then add the rice, garlic, ginger and spices. Stir to combine, add the chicken stock and season with salt and pepper.

Bring the soup to the boil, then turn the heat down to a simmer and cook until the vegetables and rice are al dente – this will take 10–12 minutes.

Add the sweet potato, greens and chicken. Cover the pan and leave the soup to cook for another 10 minutes until the sweet potato and greens are tender. Taste for seasoning and add a squeeze of lemon juice before serving.

HAIRY BIKER TIP: If you don't have any leftover chicken, you could make this soup with some cooked chicken from the supermarket.

CHICKEN ESCALOPES WITH BLACK-EYED BEANS AND GREENS

This was inspired by the fried chicken and collard greens we ate in Mississippi. It's a good idea to prepare double quantities of these escalopes and freeze them after coating with breadcrumbs. Open freeze them first on a tray, then transfer them to a container or freezer bag. It's best not to try freezing the escalopes after cooking, as they will dry out too much when reheated. You can then use your extra escalopes to make the katsu recipe on page 137. The black-eyed beans and greens also freeze surprisingly well and it's easy to make a big batch.

low-cal oil spray
(preferably olive)

2 large chicken breasts

50ml low-fat yoghurt

50g panko breadcrumbs

1 tsp oregano

1 tsp mustard powder

sea salt and black pepper

**Black-eyed beans
and greens**

1 tsp olive oil

1 onion, finely shredded

50g lean back bacon,
trimmed of fat and diced

250g spring greens,
shredded

1 tbsp tomato purée

400g can of
black-eyed beans

100g sweetcorn kernels

Preheat the oven to 200°C/Fan 180°C/Gas 6. Spritz 2 baking trays with oil. Lay a chicken breast on a board and slice into it from the side, cutting right through to make 2 flat fillets. Put each fillet between 2 sheets of cling film and flatten them with a rolling pin or meat tenderiser until they are about 5mm thick. Repeat with the other chicken breast so you have 4 thin fillets.

Put the yoghurt and breadcrumbs on separate plates. Season the crumbs and mix in the oregano and mustard powder. Dip a breast fillet into the yoghurt, making sure it is evenly coated, then press it into the panko breadcrumbs. Repeat with the remaining fillets, making sure they are all well covered. Put the coated chicken on the baking trays and spritz them with oil. Bake them for 15–20 minutes, until the chicken is cooked through and the coating has turned a light golden brown.

Meanwhile, cook the beans and greens. Heat the oil in a saucepan and add the onion and bacon. Cook until the bacon has crisped up and the onion has started to brown. Add the greens with 100ml of water and cover the pan. Leave the greens to simmer for 7–8 minutes until tender, then add the purée, beans and sweetcorn. Stir to combine and season generously. Leave to simmer, covered, for another 5 minutes until everything is heated through. Serve the chicken with the beans and greens on the side.

Serves 4 | 217 calories per serving (not including rice)
Prep: 20 minutes | Cooking time: 30 minutes

CHICKEN KATSU

This Japanese favourite is basically breaded chicken breasts served up with curry sauce.
If you've prepared some extra chicken escalopes (see page 135), this is just the thing to make
with them – or you could cook some up from scratch. Either way we guarantee you'll enjoy
this dish. Good with some steamed rice and/or some Asian greens.

4 chicken escalopes,
cooked (see p. 137)

Curry sauce
1 tsp vegetable oil
1 onion, finely chopped
2 large carrots (about
250g), finely chopped
100g button mushrooms,
roughly chopped
3 large garlic cloves,
finely chopped
30g fresh root ginger,
peeled and grated
1 tbsp medium
curry powder
500ml chicken stock
1 tsp honey
1 tbsp soy sauce
sea salt and black pepper

To make the curry sauce, heat the vegetable oil in a large
saucepan. Add the onion and carrots and cook them over
a medium heat for about 10 minutes. Keep stirring regularly,
until the vegetables are caramelising around the edges. Add
the mushrooms, garlic and ginger and continue to cook for
a further 5 minutes.

Sprinkle over the curry powder and season with salt and pepper.
Pour in the chicken stock, then add the honey and soy sauce.
Bring to the boil, then turn down the heat and simmer for
10–15 minutes until the vegetables are completely tender and
the sauce has reduced by a third.

Purée the sauce in a blender or food processor. If you want
it extra smooth, push it through a coarse sieve. Return it to the
saucepan and heat through. Taste for seasoning – add a little
more salt, pepper and honey if necessary.

Cut the cooked escalopes into strips and serve with the sauce
poured over them.

*HAIRY BIKER TIP: In Japan they serve katsu on shredded white
cabbage instead of rice. Much lower in calories.*

ROAST BEEF AND YORKSHIRE PUDDINGS

Roast beef is a treat and we find that silverside works really well and doesn't break the bank.
A 1.5–2kg joint should give you enough meat to serve six, with leftovers to make the beef ragu or
minchi another day – the meal that keeps on giving .You can't have roast beef without Yorkshires
and we suggest making double quantities and saving half to make the sweet version on page 156.

1.5–2kg beef
silverside joint
2 tsp black peppercorns
2 tsp mustard powder
1 tsp dried thyme
sea salt

Gravy
1 tbsp flour
100ml wine (red or white)
400ml beef stock
1 tsp redcurrant jelly
(optional)

Yorkshire puddings
150g plain flour
2 eggs
275ml semi-skimmed
milk

(Leftover beef and
Yorkshire puddings)

Remove the beef from the fridge at least 45 minutes before you
want to roast it so it can come up to room temperature. Set your
oven to its highest temperature. Take a note of the weight of the
beef so you can work out the roasting time.

Coarsely grind the peppercorns and mix them with the mustard
powder and thyme. Add salt, then sprinkle this mixture over the
meat until it is completely covered. Put the beef in a roasting tin,
then roast it in the preheated oven for 20 minutes.

Reduce the oven temperature to 200°C/Fan 180°C/Gas 6. Roast
the beef for 12 minutes per 500g for rare meat, 15 minutes per
500g for medium-rare, 17 minutes per 500g for medium and
20 minutes per 500g for well-done. When the meat is cooked
to your liking, remove it from the oven, place it on a warm
platter and cover it with foil. Leave it to rest for 20 minutes.

To make the gravy, strain the contents of the roasting tin into a
jug and set them aside – you will find that any fat will set quickly
and can easily be removed. Sprinkle the flour into the tin and
stir to scrape up any sticky bits from the base. Set the tin over a
medium heat and pour in the wine. Stir until the base of the tin
feels smooth, then gradually add the beef stock and the strained
contents of the tin (without the fat) to make a fairly thin gravy.

Tip the gravy into a small saucepan and add any juices from
the resting meat. Stir in the redcurrant jelly, if using, until it has
dissolved completely into the gravy.

Make the batter for the Yorkshires while the beef is cooking. Blitz all the ingredients together in a food processor until smooth, or whisk them by hand. When the beef has been removed from the oven, turn the heat up to 230°C/Fan 210°C/Gas 8 and put a 12-hole Yorkshire pudding tin into the oven to heat up.

Just before you are ready to cook the Yorkshires, carefully remove the tin and spritz the holes generously with oil. Return the tin to the oven for one minute. Divide the batter between the holes, then cook the Yorkshires in the oven for about 20 minutes until puffed up and a rich golden brown. Serve half the Yorkshire puddings with the beef and freeze the rest.

HAIRY BIKER TIPS: Leftover beef can be frozen in one piece, or sliced or diced, then frozen.

MINCHI

Minchi is like a cross between a curry and a hash with a fried egg on top - and it's a great favourite of Dave's! It comes from Macau, which is now a region of China but used to be a Portuguese territory so has a great mixture of culinary influences. The dish is traditionally made with minced beef or pork, but it is also a great way of using up leftover beef from your roast (see page 138).

1 large potato (about 250g)
2 tsp vegetable oil
1 onion, finely chopped
2 garlic cloves,
finely chopped
250g leftover roast beef,
diced, or 250g fresh mince
1 tsp Chinese five-spice
3 tbsp light soy sauce
150g peas
100g fresh baby spinach
sea salt

To garnish
low-cal oil spray
4 eggs
4 spring onions, sliced
into rounds
a few sprigs of coriander
hot sauce

Cut the potato into 1cm cubes. Bring a saucepan of water to the boil, add salt, then the potato. Cook for 2 minutes, then drain and set aside.

Heat a teaspoon of the oil in a wok. When the oil is hot and the air above it is shimmering, add the cubes of potato and stir-fry them until they're cooked through and golden brown. Remove the cubes from the wok with a slotted spoon and place them on kitchen paper to drain.

Add the second teaspoon of oil to the wok. When it's hot, add the onion. Stir-fry it over a medium heat until it's starting to take on some colour, then add the garlic and meat. Sprinkle over the five-spice and continue to cook until the meat is brown. Add the soy sauce, peas and 50ml of water and cook for 3–4 minutes.

Put the potato cubes back into the wok to heat through and stir in the spinach. When the spinach has wilted down, remove the pan from the heat.

Spray a frying pan with oil and fry the eggs until cooked to your liking. Serve the minchi with a fried egg on each serving and garnished with the spring onions and coriander. Bring some hot sauce to the table so people can add some if they want.

BEEF RAGU

This Italian-style beef sauce is a great way of using up any leftover beef from your roast and you can eke the meat out with lentils, which also add a nice variation in texture. The recipe does make quite a large quantity but it freezes well and can be used in all sorts of ways. We both love having some of this in the freezer. Take a portion out in the morning and leave it to defrost. Then in the evening, heat it up while you cook some pasta and supper is ready in no time.

low-cal oil spray (preferably olive)

500g cooked beef, diced

2 tsp olive oil

1 large onion, finely chopped

2 large carrots, finely diced

3 celery sticks, finely chopped

4 garlic cloves, finely chopped

1 tsp dried oregano

2 bay leaves

200g cooked brown lentils

250ml red wine

300ml beef stock

400g can of tomatoes

sea salt and black pepper

First take a large frying pan and spritz the base with oil. Add the beef to the pan and fry it until well browned. Remove the beef from the pan and set it aside.

Heat the 2 teaspoons of olive oil in a large pan. Add the onion, carrots and celery and fry them over a very gentle heat for 10–15 minutes, until they have started to soften. Add the garlic and herbs, then stir for a further 2 minutes. Put the beef back in the pan, add the lentils and season with salt and pepper.

Turn up the heat, pour in the wine and boil until it is reduced by about half. Add the stock and tomatoes, bring to the boil, then turn the heat down and cover the pan. Simmer for at least an hour and a half, longer if possible. Remove the lid and continue to simmer the sauce for another 20–30 minutes until it has reduced down.

Serve with pasta or leave it to cool, then divide it into portions and freeze them.

HAIRY BIKER TIP: Serve this sauce up with pasta, use it to make a cottage pie or add beans and chillies – whatever you fancy. You can, of course, also make it with ordinary minced beef and lentils.

GREEN LAMB CURRY

We've always been big fans of a curry and this one is inspired by our favourite saag gosht. Some curries can take a while to prepare but this one is no hassle, although it does need to cook for quite a while so it's good to make when you're pottering about at home. Bought curry powder is fine here or make your own using our recipe on page 182.

800g lean lamb (leg is best), trimmed of fat and diced

2½ tbsp curry powder (shop-bought or see p.182)

½ tsp salt

1 tbsp vegetable oil

2 onions, finely sliced

4 garlic cloves, finely chopped

1 tbsp tomato purée

500g fresh spinach or 1kg frozen

small bunch of coriander leaves, to serve

black pepper

Put the lamb meat in a bowl. Mix the curry powder with the salt and plenty of black pepper. Sprinkle it over the lamb and mix thoroughly until all the meat is well coated.

Heat the vegetable oil in a large flameproof casserole dish. Add the onions and cook them over a medium to low heat until they are soft and very lightly coloured. Turn up the heat and add the lamb and garlic to the casserole dish. Cook, stirring regularly, until the lamb has browned, then add the garlic and tomato purée. Stir for another couple of minutes.

Add up to 400ml of water to the dish – just enough to barely cover the lamb – then bring it to the boil. Turn down the heat to a simmer, then cover and leave the curry to cook for 1½–2 hours until the lamb is tender. Remove the lid and continue to cook for 20 minutes, uncovered, to reduce the liquid.

When the lamb has almost finished cooking, prepare the spinach. If using fresh spinach, wash it well and cook it in a large saucepan. You shouldn't need to add any additional water, just press the spinach down until it wilts. When the spinach has completely wilted down, strain off most of the liquid, then purée or finely chop it. If using frozen spinach, defrost it thoroughly and purée or finely chop it as for the fresh.

Add the spinach to the curry and stir it in thoroughly. Cook, uncovered, until the liquid has reduced down to a thick, green-flecked sauce. Serve the curry garnished with coriander and with flatbread or a portion of rice or cauliflower rice (see p.180).

Serves 4 | 418 calories per serving | Prep: 15 minutes | Cooking time: about 1 hour

LAMB AND LENTIL MEATBALLS

Meatballs are always a family favourite and this recipe satisfies even the most voracious doner lover. Make the full batch of meatballs and use half for this recipe, served up with pitta bread, salad and sauce. Freeze the rest and use them another day for the meatball tagine on page 149. Good idea or what? You'll find some more info on freezing the meatballs on page 149.

100g brown lentils
½ tsp salt
1 tsp olive oil
1 onion, finely chopped
2 garlic cloves, finely chopped or grated
1 tbsp ras-el-hanout
1 tbsp dried mint
500g lean lamb mince
1 egg
30g panko breadcrumbs
sea salt and black pepper

Sauce
200ml low-fat yogurt
1 tbsp dried mint
1 tsp ground cumin
small bunch of parsley, chopped, a few leaves reserved for garnish

To serve
4 large pitta breads
¼ red cabbage, shredded
¼ cucumber, sliced
½ red onion, finely sliced
pickled chillies or hot sauce (optional)

Rinse the lentils thoroughly under cold running water and put them in a pan. Cover them with plenty of cold water and season with the salt. Bring to the boil, then simmer the lentils, uncovered, for 25–30 minutes. They should be soft but not collapsing. Drain well, then put them in a bowl and leave to cool.

Preheat the oven to 200°C/Fan 180°C/Gas 6. Heat the oil in a frying pan, add the onion and cook it until soft, then add the garlic. Continue to cook for another minute or so, then add the onion and garlic to the lentils. Add the remaining meatball ingredients and season with salt and pepper. Mix thoroughly – the mixture may feel soft at first but will firm up as you mix.

Form the mixture into 40g torpedo-shaped balls – you should have 24. If you are cooking them all straight away, spread them over a couple of baking trays. If you are just cooking half, they should fit on one tray. Roast the meatballs in the preheated oven for 15 minutes or until well browned. They may remain slightly pink in the middle, but if you want them cooked through completely, cook for a further 5 minutes.

Blitz the sauce ingredients in a small food processor. Season with salt and pepper and tip it into a serving bowl. Toast the pittas slightly to soften them, then split them down the sides. Slice the meatballs in half and divide them between the pittas. Add cabbage, cucumber, red onion and the reserved parsley leaves to each one, then drizzle over some of the green sauce. Serve with pickled chillies or some hot sauce if you like.

MEATBALL TAGINE WITH COUSCOUS

If you've made the meatballs on the previous page, here is another great way to use them. The tagine is perfect served with this couscous, delicately flavoured with orange and herbs.

1 tsp olive oil

1 red onion, sliced into thin wedges

2 garlic cloves, finely chopped

30g fresh root ginger, grated

pinch of saffron, soaked in a little warm water

400g can of tomatoes

1 tsp honey

12 cooked meatballs

200g frozen peas

sea salt and black pepper

Couscous

125g wholemeal couscous

juice of 1 orange

1 tsp olive oil

small bunch of mint or parsley

Heat the olive oil in a large flameproof casserole dish. Add the onion and sauté it until it's starting to soften – you don't want it to collapse. Add the garlic and ginger and cook for a further minute or so, then pour in the saffron and its soaking water. Pour in the tomatoes, then swill out the can with 100ml of water and add this too. Stir in the honey and season with salt and pepper.

Add the meatballs to the casserole dish and bring everything to the boil. Cover and simmer for 10 minutes, then remove the lid and add the peas. Continue to cook, uncovered, for another 5 minutes until the peas are just cooked through and the sauce has reduced a little.

Meanwhile, prepare the couscous according to the packet instructions, using orange juice in place of some of the liquid. Season the couscous with salt and pepper, then drizzle with olive oil. Serve the couscous with the tagine and sprinkle some finely chopped mint or parsley over the top.

HAIRY BIKER TIPS: There are several different ways you can freeze these meatballs. Freeze the meatball mixture as it is, then defrost thoroughly, form into meatballs and cook as in the recipes.

Alternatively, shape the meatballs and open freeze them on a baking tray, uncooked. Once they are frozen, tip them into a freezer bag.

Or cook the meatballs, then freeze them once cool. This is fine if you are going to use them in the tagine, as they reheat well that way.

Dieting or not, we all have a fancy for something sweet once in a while. These puddings and cakes are all very easy to make but none the less tasty for that. Some are surprisingly low in calories and even the more indulgent ones are fine when paired with a lower-calorie main meal so you can have your cake and eat it. Enjoy!

EASY PEASY PUDS

Serves 4 | 166 calories per serving
Prep: 5 minutes, plus cooling | **Cooking time:** about 10 minutes

RHUBARB CUSTARD POTS

Rhubarb and custard go together perfectly – like us! This is a scrumptiously delicious version of the partnership but with a calorie count that makes it possible for dieters to enjoy. You can make these in ramekins or little cups but they look prettiest in glasses so you can see the layers.

500g rhubarb, cut into
3cm lengths
juice and zest of ½ orange
1 tbsp caster sugar
400ml low-fat custard
20–40g soft dark
brown sugar
1 tsp ground ginger

Put the rhubarb, orange juice and zest and the caster sugar in a saucepan. Cook over a low heat, stirring gently, until the sugar has dissolved. Once the rhubarb is simmering, cover the pan and leave the rhubarb to cook for 5 minutes. It should be tender but still holding its shape.

Using a slotted spoon, carefully divide the rhubarb between 4 glasses or ramekins. Try to avoid including too much of the cooking liquid. Leave to cool.

Top the cooled rhubarb with the custard. Mix the sugar and ginger together. When you are almost ready to serve, sprinkle the sugar and ginger over the custard – use more or less sugar depending on the sweetness of your rhubarb. Leave for a few minutes until the sugar has dissolved into a rich caramel-coloured pool on top of each pot.

HAIRY BIKER TIP: We love cooking but we do live in the real world and we think there's nothing wrong with the ready-made low-fat custard from the supermarket. It's great in this pud.

Serves 6 | 273 calories per serving | **Prep:** 10 minutes
Cooking time: 10 minutes (or 20–25 minutes if cooking the Yorkshires from scratch)

YORKSHIRE PUDDINGS WITH APPLE COMPOTE

We love Yorkshires and there's no reason to keep them just for roast beef. They're great served as a dessert too, with some fruit such as these fab spicy, buttery apples – think of them as a being a lovely big crispy pancake. Yorkshires freeze really well so it's always a good idea to make plenty, then freeze some for another time.

10g butter

4 eating apples, peeled and cut into wedges

1 tsp cinnamon

¼ tsp cloves

6 cooked Yorkshire puddings (see p.138)

To serve

1 tbsp maple syrup per person

1 tbsp half-fat crème fraiche per person

Preheat the oven to 200°C/Fan 180°C/Gas 6.

Heat the butter in a large frying pan or saucepan. Add the apple wedges and spices, then 2 tablespoons of water. Cover and cook the apples for about 5 minutes, shaking the pan regularly, until they are tender but still holding their shape.

Warm the Yorkshire puddings through in the preheated oven for 5 minutes. Serve them with the apples, a drizzle of maple syrup and a tablespoon of crème fraiche.

APPLE AND CINNAMON STRUDEL

If you've any filo pastry left from making the spinach and ham strudel on page 83 this is the way to use it up. Strudels look really impressive but this is one is so easy to make. And if you decide you really want to spoil yourself, serve the strudel with some half-fat crème fraiche or custard!

1 large Bramley apple
(about 500g peeled
weight), diced

50g raisins

1 tsp cinnamon

pinch of ground cloves

1 tbsp cornflour

50g light soft brown sugar

5 large sheets of filo pastry
(30 x 40cm)

low-cal oil spray
(preferably sunflower)

Put the diced apple and raisins in a large bowl. Mix the cinnamon, cloves and cornflour with the sugar and sprinkle over the apple and raisins. Stir thoroughly until the dry ingredients have completely coated the apple. Preheat the oven to 200°C/Fan 180°C/Gas 6.

Lay out a sheet of filo on a work surface and spritz it a couple of times with oil. Use a pastry brush to spread the oil over the pastry, then repeat until you have a pile of all 5 sheets. (If your filo sheets are smaller, just overlap a couple of smaller ones slightly to get roughly the right size.)

Spoon the filling along the centre of the pastry, lengthways, then brush all the edges with water. Fold the shorter edges in first, then the longer sides. Turn the strudel over so the joins are on the bottom. Spray it again with the oil spray, then transfer to a baking tray.

Cook the strudel in the oven for 25–30 minutes until the pastry has lightly browned and the filling is piping hot. Serve hot or at room temperature.

GINGER PARKIN

We loved this as kids and in our new recipe we've cut the sugar down as much as we can – it's still lovely and sweet though. Parkin is even better a couple of days after it's made so if you can, leave it for a day or two before tucking in. Cut it into small squares and test your self-discipline.

low-cal oil spray
200g self-raising flour
150g oatmeal
2 tbsp ground ginger
pinch of salt
200g soft figs, stems trimmed, finely chopped
100g butter
50g golden syrup
50g black treacle
75g light soft brown sugar
75ml milk
½ tsp bicarbonate of soda
2 eggs

Preheat the oven to 180°C/Fan 160°C/Gas 4. Line a 20–22cm square baking tin with baking paper, or spray it with low-cal oil.

Put the flour, oatmeal and ground ginger in a bowl with a pinch of salt and whisk to combine. Set aside.

Put the chopped figs into a saucepan with 200ml of water. Bring to the boil, then turn the heat down to a simmer. Mash the figs into the water while the mixture reduces and becomes like a runny syrup. Add the butter, golden syrup, treacle and sugar and leave to melt. Pour in the milk, then sprinkle over the bicarbonate of soda. Wait for the mixture to foam up a little, then remove the pan from the heat.

Beat the eggs, one at a time, into the contents of the saucepan, then gently fold in the dry ingredients. Scrape the mixture into your prepared tin and then bake for about 30 minutes. The cake should be firm but spongy to the touch and have shrunken away slightly from the sides. Remove it from the oven and leave to cool in the tin.

Once the parkin is cold, cut it into squares and store it in an airtight tin. It keeps well for a couple of weeks.

MANGO FOOL

Mango makes one of the best of all fools we think. No cooking, just a little mixing and you have something that's fragrantly delicious. Super simple, super fresh, super tasty.

300g diced mango
zest and juice of 1 lime
100ml double cream
200ml 0% fat Greek
yoghurt
2 tsp icing sugar

Put 150g of the mango into a food processor with half the lime zest and juice. Blitz until smooth, then set aside.

Finely dice the remaining mango and mix it with the rest of the lime juice. Divide the diced mango between 4 ramekins or glass dishes.

Put the double cream into a large bowl. Whisk until it has increased in volume and is soft and billowy – do not overwhip as you don't want the cream to be too stiff. Fold in the yoghurt and the icing sugar, followed by the puréed mango. Stir until the mango is completely combined or leave it with swirls of orange and white – up to you.

Add the creamy mango mixture to the dishes and sprinkle with the remaining zest. Chill the fools until you're ready to serve.

PEACH AND RASPBERRY TRIFLE

It's what we've always dreamed of – a glorious trifle for dieters. We've kept the stodge to a minimum, used shop-bought low-fat custard and yoghurt and we think we've come up with a winner. Make this with fresh peaches or canned, and if you use canned you could substitute half the wine or sherry with the juice. You might have this instead of supper but it's so worth it.

12 amaretti biscuits
100ml sweet dessert wine or sherry
3 peaches, sliced into wedges (peeled if you like)
250g raspberries
500ml low-fat custard
100ml double cream
200ml 0% fat Greek yoghurt
1 tbsp icing sugar
25g flaked almonds

Put the amaretti biscuits in the base of a trifle bowl. Pour over the sweet dessert wine or sherry.

Arrange the peach slices and raspberries over the biscuits, then pour over the custard. Whisk the double cream until it has increased in volume but is still quite soft, then mix it with the yoghurt and icing sugar. Spoon this on to the trifle, cover and leave it in the fridge to chill until you are almost ready to serve.

Put the flaked almonds into a dry frying pan and toast them until lightly coloured all over. Tip the almonds on to a plate and leave them to cool, then sprinkle them over the trifle just before serving.

CHERRY CLAFOUTIS

Clafoutis is a French dessert of fruit cooked in a lovely custard-like batter. The classic version is made with cherries but many other kinds of fruit can be used instead if you prefer. Simple and quick to make and delicious to eat.

350g cherries, pitted
15g caster sugar
30ml kirsch (optional)
5g butter
1 tbsp demerara sugar

Batter
75g plain flour
25g caster sugar
pinch of salt
2 eggs
200ml whole milk
50ml half-fat crème fraiche
a few drops of almond extract (optional)

To serve
half-fat crème fraiche

Put the cherries in a bowl and sprinkle the sugar and the kirsch, if using, over them. Leave the cherries to macerate for about half an hour.

Preheat the oven to 180°C/Fan 160°C/Gas 4. Grease a shallow ovenproof dish with the butter, then sprinkle over the demerara sugar. Drain the cherries and spread them evenly over the base of the dish.

For the batter, put the flour in a bowl with the sugar and salt. Whisk in the eggs, then add the milk and crème fraiche. Stir in the almond extract, if using. Pour the batter into the dish around the cherries. You may find the cherries start floating at this point so push them back into place if they move around too much.

Bake the clafoutis for 25–30 minutes, until the batter is a rich golden brown and slightly puffed up. Serve with a spoonful of crème fraiche.

HAIRY BIKER TIP: You can make this with canned or frozen cherries when fresh ones aren't around. Just drain them really well and pat them dry, otherwise there will be too much liquid.

APRICOT COBBLER

A cobbler can be sweet or savoury and has a topping of a sort of scone-like mixture on top – it's a very popular dish in the US. The topping turns this into a really filling pud so pair it with a low-cal soup or salad to balance your calories. You could use fresh fruit, of course, but a can is so easy and means you can make this at any time of year.

400g can of apricot halves
in juice, drained
2 tbsp light soft
brown sugar
1 tsp cinnamon
pinch of salt

Topping
150g self-raising flour
½ tsp baking powder
25g caster sugar
pinch of salt
100ml buttermilk
1 tsp vanilla extract
1 egg

Preheat the oven to 180°C/Fan 160°C/Gas 4. Put the apricots in the base of an ovenproof dish. Sprinkle over the sugar, cinnamon and a pinch of salt, then mix to combine. Set aside.

For the topping, put the flour, baking powder and sugar into a bowl with a pinch of salt and mix thoroughly. Whisk the buttermilk, vanilla extract and egg together until well combined, then stir this mixture into the dry ingredients to make a slightly sticky dough, similar to that of dumplings.

Dot heaped tablespoons of the topping over the apricots. Bake the cobbler in the preheated oven for 30–35 minutes until cooked through. Serve with half-fat crème fraiche or custard if you like but don't forget to count the calories.

HAIRY BIKER TIPS: You'll find buttermilk in supermarkets but if you don't have any, put a tablespoon of lemon juice in a jug and top it up with milk to 100ml. Leave it for 5 minutes before using.

Also you can freeze the cobbler in individual ramekins. Let them defrost, then cook for 20–25 minutes.

Serves 6 | 144 calories per serving | Prep: 15 minutes
Cooking time: 10 minutes (but does need to be left for several hours or overnight)

WINTER PUDDING

We love summer pudding so much that we thought, why leave such a wonderful thing for just one season of the year? So we came up with a superb autumn/winter version that we hope you will like as much as we do. A fruity igloo of joy.

low-cal oil spray

6 slices of bread, crusts removed

2 eating apples, peeled and diced

400g blackberries

200g cranberries

1 tsp ground cinnamon

½ tsp ground ginger

pinch of ground cloves

2 tbsp caster sugar

half-fat crème fraiche, to serve

Spray a 900ml pudding basin with oil, then line it with cling film. Cut a round from one of the slices of bread and place it in the base of the pudding basin. Cut the remaining slices into thirds and arrange these around the sides of the bowl, overlapping them slightly. Press the bread down against the bowl. You should have 2 or 3 slices left for the top.

Put the fruit in a saucepan and sprinkle over the spices and sugar. Add 50ml of water and heat slowly, stirring gently until the sugar dissolves. Simmer until the cranberries have plumped up and are close to bursting. At this point the fruit should have given out a lot of juice and created a deep reddish-purple sauce.

Ladle some of the sauce into the pudding basin so it can soak through the bread, then, using a slotted spoon, add the fruit to the basin. Slowly pour in all the juice, giving it time to soak in as you do so. Fold in any bread that is left exposed, then top with the remaining slices.

Place a saucer on top of the pudding and weigh it down with something heavy – a can of beans or tomatoes works well. Put the pudding in the fridge and leave it for several hours, but preferably overnight.

To serve, place a serving plate upside down on top of the basin and turn the pudding out on to the plate. Peel off the cling film. Serve with half-fat crème fraiche.

LEMON AND BLUEBERRY MUG CAKES

Sometimes you get an irresistible urge for a sweet hit and you just need cake.
These are ready in a few minutes and they really satisfy the craving.

2 tsp butter, melted
1 egg
1 tbsp lemon juice
zest of ½ lemon
1 tbsp 0% fat yoghurt
3 tbsp self-raising flour
2 tbsp caster sugar
pinch of salt
30g blueberries
1 tbsp half-fat crème
fraiche, to serve (optional)

Using a fork, whisk the melted butter with the egg in a bowl.
Add the lemon juice and zest and the yoghurt, then whisk in
the flour, sugar and a pinch of salt, making sure you get rid of
any lumps. Stir in three-quarters of the blueberries.

Divide the mixture between 2 teacups and sprinkle the rest of
the blueberries on top. Place the cups on a plate to catch any
overflow. Cook the cakes in a microwave on high for about
1 minute and 15 seconds, then check to see if they are done –
they should have risen and be firm to the touch. If necessary,
cook them for a little longer. Microwave timings do vary from
oven to oven , though, so use your judgement and see what
works best for you.

Eat the cakes straight from the cups with half a tablespoon
of crème fraiche if you like. It will add another 12 calories to
each serving.

CHEWY ORANGE AND RAISIN COOKIES

We have to watch our biscuit habit but these are reasonably low cal and at least if you make your own you know exactly what you're eating. They're dead tasty too.

250g plain flour
1½ tsp baking powder
pinch of salt
85g melted butter, slightly cooled
2 egg whites
1 tbsp milk
zest of ½ large orange
1 tsp vanilla extract
175g light soft brown sugar
75g raisins

Put the flour and baking powder into a bowl and add a pinch of salt. Pour the melted butter into a separate bowl and add the egg whites. Whisk for a minute to combine, then add the milk, orange zest, vanilla extract and sugar. Mix together thoroughly, then pour this mixture into the bowl of dry ingredients and add the raisins. Mix everything together, trying not to overwork it, and you should end up with a slightly sticky dough.

Cover the dough with cling film and leave it to chill for at least an hour or so.

When you are ready to bake the cookies, preheat the oven to 160°C/Fan 140°C/Gas 3. Form the dough into 24 balls and arrange them on a couple of baking trays. Press each cookie down lightly to a thickness of about 1cm.

Bake the cookies in the oven for 12–15 minutes until they are just starting to take on some colour. They will spread out but they might still seem a little undercooked when you take them out of the oven. Leave them on the baking tray and they will firm up as they cool. They will keep in an airtight container for several days.

HAIRY BIKER TIP: You can freeze the dough as it is or after shaping it into cookies. If freezing as cookies, open freeze them on a baking tray first, then tip them into a bag or container. After freezing, defrost them before cooking or cook from frozen for 18–20 minutes.

CHOCOLATE RICE PUDDING

Ahem, now this is a treat. We love rice pudding and we love chocolate and the two of them together make proper comfort food heaven. You could serve some tangerine segments on the side to get a kind of chocolate-orange vibe.

100g short-grain (pudding) rice
600ml whole milk
½ tsp vanilla extract
30g cocoa powder
2 tbsp caster sugar
25g dark chocolate, peeled into curls

Put the rice in a pan with 500ml of the milk and the vanilla extract. Bring the milk almost to the boil, then turn the heat down and leave it to simmer over a medium to low heat for up to 20 minutes until the rice is almost tender. Keep a close eye on the milk and make sure it doesn't come to the boil or boil over.

Whisk the remaining milk with the cocoa and sugar until thoroughly combined. Stir this into the rice and continue to cook for another 10 minutes, stirring regularly to make sure the mixture doesn't catch on the bottom of the pan.

Remove the pan from the heat and leave the rice pudding to stand for a few minutes. Serve it hot or cold, sprinkled with chocolate curls.

We've wanted to keep things easy in this book and we've used ready-made curry powder, shop-bought stocks and so on. But sometimes you might want to go the extra mile and make your own so we've included a few recipes for these basics. Trick is to make a big batch of stock, curry paste or whatever and stash it in the freezer. That way you can save time and money.

BASICS

PITTA BREADS

Yes, you can buy pittas in the corner shop but it's well worth making your own when you have time. And you can also use this dough to make our wonderful tartlets (see page 79). The dough is best frozen after the first rise and then defrosted naturally at room temperature. Alternatively, freeze the pittas after baking and warm them through in an oven or toaster before serving.

250g strong white bread flour, plus extra for dusting
2 tsp instant yeast
1 tbsp olive oil
½ tsp salt
pinch of sugar
150ml tepid water

Mix all the ingredients until everything comes together in a ball, then turn out the dough out on to a lightly floured surface. Knead the dough until it is soft and pliable – this will take up to 10 minutes. Alternatively, use a stand mixer with a dough hook if you have one available.

Put the dough back into a bowl and cover it with a damp tea towel or cling film. Leave it somewhere warm for at least an hour or until it has doubled in size.

Preheat the oven to its hottest setting and heat a couple of baking trays. Turn out the dough and cut it into 8 pieces. Form these into smooth balls, cover and leave them to rest for a further 15 minutes. Roll out each dough ball into a long oval shape and place them on the baking trays.

Bake the pittas in the oven for 6–7 minutes until they have started to colour and have puffed up.

Remove them from the oven and cover with a tea towel (this will stop them from going hard) until they have collapsed down and are cool.

CHINESE-STYLE PANCAKES

These freeze best after cooking. Be sure to dust them well with flour before stacking them up, then wrap them tightly so no condensation can get in.

150g plain flour, plus extra
for dusting
pinch of salt
120ml freshly boiled water
low-cal oil spray

Put the flour into a bowl with a pinch of salt. Gradually stir in the water to make a sticky, flaky ball of dough, then turn this out on to a floured surface. Knead until you have a smooth dough.

Put the dough in a bowl, cover and leave it to rest for half an hour. Cut it into 12 pieces, roll each piece into a ball, then spray them with oil. Roll each ball out into a thin pancake. Dust the pancakes with flour so they don't stick to each other.

To cook, heat a frying pan and cook the pancakes over a medium to low heat for 1–2 minutes on each side. You may see some steam coming off them to start with and the dough will turn from matt to almost transparent before setting. Wrap the pancakes in a tea towel to keep them warm.

To reheat, either wrap the pancakes in foil and put them in a warm oven for 15–20 minutes, or heat them through in a steamer for a few minutes.

CAULIFLOWER RICE

Use this for the avocado poke bowl recipe on page 48 or serve it with curries, casseroles or any other dish you would usually eat with rice. You'll find it soaks up juices beautifully without loading you with calories.

1 medium cauliflower (about 600g), broken into florets
low-cal oil spray
sea salt and black pepper

Put the cauliflower florets in a food processor and blitz until they're the consistency of breadcrumbs. Spray a large frying pan with oil, add the cauliflower and toast it for a minute or so, while stirring. Season with salt and pepper.

Add about 100ml of water to the pan and cook the cauliflower for about 5 minutes until all the water has been absorbed, stirring frequently. The cauliflower should be tender but still with a little bite to it.

If you like, you can add chopped fresh herbs, fried onions, flaked almonds or spices to the cauliflower.

TANDOORI PASTE

This is a beautifully fragrant spicy paste and it's well worth mixing some of this up when you have a moment and stashing it in the freezer. We like Kashmiri chilli powder but you can use any mild to medium red chilli powder, depending on the level of heat you like.

1–2 tbsp Kashmiri chilli powder
1 tbsp ground cumin
1 tbsp ground coriander
2 tsp ground cardamom
1 tsp ground turmeric
1 tsp ground fenugreek
½ tsp ground cinnamon
½ tsp cayenne
2 tbsp tomato purée
50g fresh root ginger, peeled and grated
4 garlic cloves, crushed or grated
juice of 1 lemon
sea salt and black pepper

Mix all the spices together in a bowl, then work them into the tomato purée until you have a very thick paste. Add the ginger, garlic and lemon juice, then season with salt and pepper.

Use the paste immediately or store it in a jar iin the fridge for up to a week.

The paste can also be frozen. Roll it into tablespoon-sized balls and open freeze them on a baking tray until solid, then transfer them to a bag or box.

QUICK CURRY POWDER

Instead of using whole spices we're suggesting ground here to make this really quick and easy. Takes no time to do and will give your curries a special kick.

2 tbsp ground cumin
2 tbsp ground coriander
1 tbsp ground turmeric
1 tbsp ground cardamom
2 tsp ground cinnamon
1 tsp ground white pepper
1 tsp ground fenugreek
¼ tsp ground cloves
¼ tsp ground nutmeg
1 tsp cayenne

Simply mix all the spices together and transfer the curry powder to a small airtight jar. That's it!

VEGETABLE STOCK

This is a good basic vegetable stock and it's great to have in your freezer to add flavour to soups, stews and other dishes.

1 tsp olive oil

2 large onions, roughly chopped

3 large carrots, well washed, chopped

200g squash or pumpkin, unpeeled, diced

4 celery sticks, sliced

2 leeks, sliced

100ml white wine or vermouth

1 large sprig of thyme

1 large sprig of parsley

1 bay leaf

a few peppercorns

Heat the olive oil in a large saucepan. Add all the vegetables and fry them over a high heat, stirring regularly, until they're starting to brown and caramelise around the edges. This will take at least 10 minutes. Add the white wine or vermouth and boil until it has evaporated away.

Cover the veg with 2 litres of water and add the herbs and peppercorns. Bring to the boil, then turn the heat down to a gentle simmer. Cook the stock, uncovered, for about an hour, stirring every so often.

Check the stock – the colour should have some depth to it. Strain the stock through a colander or a sieve lined with muslin, kitchen paper or coffee filter paper into a bowl and store it in the fridge for up to a week. Alternatively, pour the stock into freezer-proof containers and freeze.

CHICKEN STOCK

This is a great stock to make with your roast chicken carcass and if you like, you can save a few carcasses up in the freezer to make a larger quantity of stock. You can store the stock in the fridge for up to four days, or you can freeze it.

2 onions, unpeeled
and quartered
2 carrots, roughly
chopped
1 tbsp olive oil
1–3 chicken carcasses
1 sprig of thyme
2 celery sticks, roughly
chopped
a few peppercorns
1 bay leaf
parsley stems

Preheat the oven to its highest temperature. Put the onions and carrots in a roasting tin and drizzle them with the oil, then roast them until they are starting to char. Alternatively, you can do this in a pan on the hob. The idea is to caramelise the vegetables to enrich the stock.

Break the chicken carcasses up a little, then put them in a saucepan with the remaining ingredients and cover with water. Use up to a litre for one carcass and up to 1.5 litres for 2 or 3, but don't add so much water that the chicken is floating around. It needs to be quite a snug fit. Bring the water to the boil and skim off any mushroom-coloured foam that collects on top. Keep skimming until the foam turns white, then turn down the heat and cover the pan. Simmer the stock very gently for 1½–2 hours.

Strain the stock through a sieve lined with kitchen paper or muslin, but don't push the bits through if you want a clear stock. Discard all the solids. Leave the stock to cool to room temperature, then chill it in the fridge. When it is cold, you can remove any fat that's sitting on top.

HAIRY BIKER TIP: You can reduce the stock down further to get a more concentrated flavour and freeze it in ice-cube trays. Once the cubes are frozen, turn them out into a plastic bag or container and store in the freezer.

CHEERS GANG!

We love making our cookbooks and we love all the people who help us put them together. First off, thanks to the wonderful Catherine Phipps who has helped us create what we think is an exceptional batch of recipes. Andrew Hayes-Watkins, as always, has taken amazing photos for us. Mima Sinclair and her assistant Jemima O'Lone are new members of the team and we'd like to welcome them and say big thanks for cooking the food for the pictures so beautifully. And thanks to Tamzin Ferdinando for providing some great pots and pans to put it all in.

Abi Hartshorne has done us proud with the design, and many thanks yet again to our editor Jinny Johnson for her unending support, work and friendship. Love and thanks to the fab Amanda Harris, our publisher, and Lucie Stericker, creative director, for their wisdom and guidance. Thanks also to Elise See Tai for proofreading, Vicki Robinson for the index and to Fiona Hunter for the nutritional info and advice.

Love to all at James Grant for your help and support – our management team: Natalie Zietcer, Holly Pye, Lizzie Barroll Brown and Emma Rigarlsford; and our lovely literary agents: Rowan Lawton and Eugenie Furniss.

COOKING NOTES

We've given calorie counts for all our dishes. Be sure to follow the recipes carefully so you don't change the totals. Weigh ingredients and use proper spoons and a measuring jug. The calorie counts do not include optional ingredients.

We know it really helps to have a well-stocked freezer so we've marked all the recipes that are suitable for freezing. It's well worth cooking up batches of these for those busy times.

We mention spray oil in quite a few recipes, as this is an easy way of reducing the amount of oil you use. Buy the most natural kind you can find and spritz it lightly. If you don't want to use spray oil, just brush on a small amount of oil with a pastry brush. Or buy a spray bottle and fill it with the oil of your choice.

Peel onions, garlic and all other vegetables and fruit unless otherwise specified.

It's great to have homemade stock in your freezer – have a look at our recipes on pages 183–184. Otherwise, use cubes, bouillon powder, stockpots or the fresh stocks available in many supermarkets now. Remember, this is all about easy, tasty food.

We'd like to dedicate this book to Amanda Harris, with much respect, love and affection. She has been a constant source of inspiration, guidance and fun for the past decade.

First published in Great Britain in 2018 by
Seven Dials, an imprint of the Orion Publishing Group Ltd
Carmelite House
50 Victoria Embankment
London EC4Y 0DZ
An Hachette UK Company

10 9 8 7 6 5 4 3 2 1

A CIP catalogue record for this book is available from the
British Library.

ISBN: 978 1 4091 7189 8

Recipe and food consultant: Catherine Phipps
Photographer: Andrew Hayes-Watkins
Food stylist: Mima Sinclair
Design and art direction: Hart Studio
Project editor: Jinny Johnson
Prop stylist: Tamzin Ferdinando
Food stylist's assistant: Jemima O'Lone
Proofreader: Elise See Tai
Indexer: Vicki Robinson

Nutritional analysis calculated by Fiona Hunter, BSc (Hons) Nutrition,
Dip Dietetics

Printed and bound in Germany

The Orion Publishing Group's policy is to use papers that are natural, renewable
and recyclable and made from wood grown in sustainable forests. The logging and
manufacturing processes are expected to conform to the environmental regulations of
the country of origin.